Forging Queer Leaders

of related interest

Trans Power
Own Your Gender
Juno Roche
ISBN 978 1 78775 019 7
eISBN 978 1 78775 020 3

The Book of Non-Binary Joy
Embracing the Power of You
Ben Pechey
ISBN 978 1 78775 910 7
eISBN 978 1 78775 911 4

Surviving Transphobia
Edited by Laura A. Jacobs
ISBN 978 1 78775 965 7
eISBN 978 1 78775 966 4

The Queer Mental Health Workbook
A Creative Self-Help Guide Using CBT, CFT and DBT
Dr. Brendan J. Dunlop
ISBN 978 1 83997 107 5
eISBN 978 1 83997 108 2

Forging Queer Leaders

How the LGBTQIA+ Community
Creates Impact from Adversity

Bree Fram and Liz Cavallaro

Jessica Kingsley Publishers
London and Philadelphia

First published in Great Britain in 2024 by Jessica Kingsley Publishers
An imprint of Hodder & Stoughton Ltd
An Hachette Company

1

Front cover image source: Shutterstock®

The scripture quotation in Chapter 2 is from the New Revised Standard Version
Bible: Anglicized Edition, copyright © 1989, 1995 National Council of the Churches
of Christ in the United States of America. Used by permission. All rights reserved.

Content warning: This book contains mention of homophobia and transphobia.

Disclaimer: The views expressed are those of the authors and do not reflect the
official guidance or position of the United States Government, the Department
of Defense, the United States Navy, or the United States Space Force.

A CIP catalogue record for this title is available from the
British Library and the Library of Congress

ISBN 978 1 83997 839 5
eISBN 978 1 83997 840 1

Printed and bound in the United States by Integrated Books International

Jessica Kingsley Publishers' policy is to use papers that are natural,
renewable and recyclable products and made from wood grown in
sustainable forests. The logging and manufacturing processes are expected
to conform to the environmental regulations of the country of origin.

Jessica Kingsley Publishers
Carmelite House
50 Victoria Embankment
London EC4Y 0DZ

www.jkp.com

Contents

Acknowledgements

We have to start by thanking the many contributors to this book who provided interviews or written submissions, and the guests who have appeared on our *Forged in Fire: LGBTQ+ Leadership* Podcast. While there was no way to squeeze in all the incredible content from them that we would like to have shared, their inputs were invaluable, and we learned from each and every one of them. This book was in no way possible without them dedicating their time, passion, and thoughtfulness when responding to all of our questions. We cannot thank them enough.

We'd also like to thank Alex DiFrancesco, Blake Dremann, Brittany Bell Connolly, Katie McNamara, Tahina Montoya, and Mark Wernersbach for their early reviews. Their insightful suggestions made this book so much more succinct and impactful. We greatly appreciate the time and talent of Jaimee Freeman who captured our author photo for this book. Finally, thanks to the team at Jessica Kingsley Publishers for making the space for books that might not otherwise be published and for taking a chance on us.

Bree wrote this book during a period of major health challenges in her family, including her own battle with cancer, and would like to thank the unwavering support given to her by the United States Space Force and leaders such as Brian Shannon and Erin Carper, who she was lucky enough to work for at the time. The culture being built by the Space Force, centered around good leadership that takes care of people and allows them to reach their full potential as their authentic selves, exemplifies so many of the key takeaways of this book.

Bree would also like to thank her wife, Peg, and children, Can and Alivya, for their support, inspiration, and for letting her get away with so much time at the keyboard. She's also grateful to the teaching team and her classmates from the *Leadership Development Course* at the Naval War College where she wrote the precursor paper that became the seed for this book. Most importantly, that's where she connected with Liz, who enthusiastically said "Yes!!" to writing this book together. It has been an absolute joy to work with her. Lastly, Bree is always thankful for, and inspired by, the thousands of transgender members of the military. Despite uncertainty and shifting tides regarding their future, they have embraced their authenticity and stand on guard to protect the opportunity for everyone else to live in freedom and embrace their full potential.

Liz began this writing journey with deep gratitude for the opportunity to blend her professional passion in leader development with a lifelong, personal passion for LGBTQ+ advocacy and allyship. She would like to thank the mentors who encouraged the pursuit of passion and purpose, especially Dr. Neal Chalofsky, who taught her the importance of meaningful work, and Dr. Olenda Johnson, who provided a constant source of light and inspiration.

She'd like to express her gratitude and admiration for Bree in bringing the fortitude and energy necessary to ensure the success and positive impact of this passion project. Liz learned that saying "Yes" to this journey was the best lesson she's ever had in trusting her instincts and aligning with the right people to advance the right message.

She'd also like to thank her mother for teaching her kindness and acceptance, her husband Hank for providing unwavering love and support, and her niece Madison for being the inspiration to create a better future.

Preface

Notes to Readers

Reading this book

If you're a cover-to-cover reader, dive right in and skip this section. But if you like to jump around, or just hit the relevant bits for you, reading this Preface might save you some time. This book provides a coherent narrative, with threads woven throughout, and is best read in full to get the whole narrative. However, the three parts of the book are also fairly distinct, so here's a quick guide. Part I answers the question of why. It is the background, history, theory, and context, putting LGBTQ+ leadership in perspective, and provides a richer experience for understanding the rest of the content. Part II explains how LGBTQ+ leaders, through their formative, often negative, experiences, develop leadership superpowers. It is rich in story and the experiences of contributors from diverse backgrounds. Part III is the "why it matters" section. It contains practical guidance for leaders to leverage the powers LGBTQ+ individuals bring to organizations, talks about why LGBTQ+ leadership development is relevant for all people, and explores the power of inclusion. Dig in!

Inclusive language

Throughout this book we use the term LGBTQ+ for readability and to represent all the diversity that exists within the spectrums of sexual orientation and gender identity aside from heterosexual and cisgender. If a contributor used another term in their quote we retained their original language. Language in this area frequently changes as our understanding grows so we recognize there's no perfect term we can use.

Quotes

If a quote doesn't have an associated footnote it's from one of the contributors to this work. Our contributors shared with us through questionnaires, interviews, long-form stories, and as guests on the Forged in Fire: LGBTQ+ Leadership Development Podcast.[1] Their quotes have been lightly edited for clarity and readability. All other quotes are referenced.

PART 1

The LGBTQ+ Leader

CHAPTER I

Introduction

Navy Lieutenant Junior Grade Kris Moore had just been hit by a thunderbolt launched through Twitter. Unbeknownst to him, as his ship sat in port in July 2017, President Trump began typing out a series of tweets. He tweeted, "After consultation with my Generals and military experts, please be advised that the United States Government will not accept or allow..."[1] The world held its breath for eight minutes before the president tweeted again. At the time, tensions were high with North Korea and the fear of nuclear escalation seemed to be at a post-Cold War peak. Yet, there was to be no war with North Korea. The president finished his thought about what the United States could not accept: transgender people in the military. People like Kris Moore.

Kris faced significant adversity in his career based on his identity. Having enlisted prior to the repeal of the Don't Ask, Don't Tell (DADT) law in 2011, he hid the fact that he was attracted to women, something not allowed for a person the Navy perceived to be female. Still, he persevered and earned a coveted appointment to the Naval Academy. Although able to come out as a lesbian in his sophomore year following the repeal of DADT, it would not be the last time Kris went through the crucible experience of coming out.

Kris graduated from the academy and was assigned to his

first ship as a surface warfare officer. In late 2015, as the Pentagon was considering policy updates to allow transgender people to serve, Kris once again came up against institutional barriers to his authenticity. Despite that, he came out again as a transgender man. He gave a speech to the assembled officers of his ship, all of whom were senior to him, and closed by asking if anyone had any questions. The only one came from the chief engineer: "Are you happy?" Kris nodded yes. Loudly, the chief proclaimed, "Then who cares what anyone else has to say?" Questions were over.

In 2017 the adversity Kris previously faced was back and this time it was coming directly from his commander-in-chief. Kris' ability to serve was again being questioned based not on his performance or potential, but solely based on who he was—he just didn't know it yet. His ship quietly rocked by the pier on a beautiful summer morning as the Twitter hurricane approached. By midday, it reached the ship. An announcement went out over ship-wide broadcast asking Kris to report to the Captain's cabin; it was almost never good news if a junior officer had to report there. Kris arrived and the captain asked him to sit before he turned on the TV. Kris went numb and could barely hear what was being said around him as the words slowly scrolled across the bottom of the screen: Trump to ban transgender service members from serving in military.[2] As statements of support from others in the room began to fall from their lips, Kris felt emotion well up and asked to be excused.

Kris recalls his thoughts and plans from that moment after returning to his stateroom. "I said hell no. I'm not going to quit. I cried...*a lot*, but I wasn't about to lay down and let them walk over me. I worked harder and studied more. I wanted to prove that if they were going to kick me out, they were going to lose the best surface warfare officer the Navy had." Kris' resilience and grit had to grow by leaps and bounds. He said, "I became so focused on achieving my goals that nearly nothing could hold me back... I have learned to improvise, adapt, and overcome. Being a minority has taught me a level of determination you can't achieve without significant adversity." Four years later, in the summer of 2021 Lieutenant Moore completed a tour as a leadership instructor at the Naval Academy and began training to serve as a department head on a new ship. He's had ample opportunities to put what he learned into practice and to shape soon-to-be naval officers into future leaders.

Kris' story is just one example of an LGBTQ+ leader overcoming adversity and going through crucible moments on their leadership journey. The journeys of leaders like Kris have a lot to teach all of us. We use stories like his to highlight the contributions LGBTQ+ leaders make to their organizations, explore how they develop uncommon leadership superpowers that perfectly fit our world, and demonstrate how all of us can benefit from their experiences and leadership.

Why We Wrote This Book

An important question any author asks is "Why am I writing this book?" So why us, why now, and why the topic of LGBTQ+ leadership? There's certainly a professional interest for us. Liz is an adult development scholar and executive coach. Bree has served as president of an advocacy nonprofit and in a wide variety of military leadership roles. We came together virtually during the pandemic in 2020 and realized a massive void exists at the intersection of LGBTQ+ identity and leadership development. Amazing stories made us believe there was something unique about why and how LGBTQ+ individuals develop leadership superpowers. We wanted to explore how their journeys develop leadership skills and capacities.

We also wrote this book for incredibly personal reasons. For Bree, as a transgender military officer, the past decade has been a rollercoaster fighting for the opportunity to serve openly and authentically. Her experiences connected her with LGBTQ+ leaders willing to risk everything to do the right thing on behalf of others. She watched people who were assets to the nation thrown out of the military for who they were or for who they loved. Bree was dismayed by the country's self-inflicted wounds and the lost talent. After the events of September 11, 2001, article after article was written about Arab-speaking linguists who had been discharged for being gay.[3] What could we have learned if they had been part of a culture that accepted them and their talents? But as DADT, a law preventing open service of LGB troops, and the ban on transgender service faded away, Bree also saw people flourish in awe-inspiring ways as they served openly and authentically. Liz built her scholarship around helping leaders thrive through developing enhanced cognitive capacity. She studies and utilizes coaching, assessment, and leadership development practices designed to expand thinking and support lifelong learning and growth. She leverages these practices to support leaders facing unprecedented challenges in complex contexts and amidst constant change. Through her work, she's observed the powerful impacts of adversity on the development of leaders' personal and professional journeys. This project provided her the opportunity to combine her expertise with her personal dedication to advocacy and support of the LGBTQ+ community.

The Power of Story

As we researched and spoke with LGBTQ+ leaders, their experiences held us rapt. It's often repeated, because it's true: stories have power. Anyone who has cried through a movie, laughed at a play, or been motivated to take up a cause by the pages of a book knows story connects us with concepts and with one another. They help us sync the rational and emotional parts of ourselves. We think stories from LGBTQ+ leaders will kindle your intellectual curiosity. They'll make you think about how these people became who they are and why they've blossomed into incredible leaders. But we also think they'll connect on an emotional level, or as Bree's kids say, they'll "hit you right in the feels."

Our contributors shared heart-wrenchingly painful and soaringly hopeful narratives. They are as excited as we are to see them shared. Author, advocate, and vice president of the GLAAD Media Institute, Ross Murray talked about why stories are important:

> Advocacy work has this very educational component to it. We want people to get things intellectually. But they need to digest, absorb, believe, and feel this in their gut and in their heart. It's that initial gut reaction that drives people. We get to the joy, the anger, these really core feelings. It gets processed through our heart and then it gets made sense of in our head, but it's all based on that initial feeling. We give people feelings through our stories and then we end those stories with "Now that you're feeling something, this is what I want you to do about it."

Transgender non-commissioned officer in the Space Force, Sabrina Bruce, beautifully captured the hopes and the excitement we share. She said, "Cultural stigmatization exists around LGBT people. So by sharing stories of leadership, it helps adjust the narrative and normalize our experiences." She also described why she wanted to contribute. "This is a book about leadership. I'm excited to put it down on paper and get it out there for people to see, because we don't have enough LGBT superheroes. Maybe somebody who needs this can read it."

While this isn't a self-help book, you'll learn a lot about how great leadership can be fostered and developed. Along the way, you'll meet leaders like Sabrina who may inspire you, show you what's possible, or challenge your conceptions about LGBTQ+ individuals. Market analyst and transgender woman Dayna Walker expressed it this way: "The more positive stories we come forward with and express, the better off we're going to be. The narratives I heard for years before I publicly came out were uninspiring. It was dismal...those stories were not success stories." We'll provide a scaffolding that wraps around inspirational stories and connects them to how and why LGBTQ+ leaders develop capacities that can take us all to new heights.

After reading this book, our words might not stick with you. What we hope will stick are the stories. Michelle Macander, a lesbian Marine Corps lieutenant colonel, and the first woman to command a Marine ground combat battalion, said, "You could read facts and figures and that's not something that's going to stick in people's minds but it's the stories that really do and what actually change people's minds." If you're approaching this book skeptically, that's great; we're glad you're here! Maybe the stories will have you believing there's something special about the way LGBTQ+ people develop leadership superpowers. Learning about it can do all of us a lot of good. So while we want to educate and make the case for inclusion, it'll be our contributors' stories driving the points home.

Why Deliberately Explore LGBTQ+ Leadership

Asked why her journey to authenticity was important to understand, DEI (diversity, equality, and inclusion) thought leader, author, and entrepreneur Jennifer Brown said:

> What does it create in us when we have to fight in the closet, and when we have to fight our way out of it? What does it grow in us? What does it ignite in us? It ignites this commitment to ourselves that is tested, but prevails. That's a huge victory. It's a power. It's a light you ignite in yourself that never goes out. It's a belief in yourself. It's a faith in the rightness of you. We can be so powerful, so persuasive, so empathetic, so perceptive. We can be such gifted leaders precisely because of these struggles and the survival that it took to be us. There's something very beautiful out of that. I credit coming out with a lot of my courage, resilience, and character. I don't know if I ever would have been the person I am now if that had not been who I was.

Journeys like Jennifer's are what we seek to understand. How do LGBTQ+ experiences forge amazing leaders?

This book is predicated on an idea: good leadership helps all of us flourish. With good leadership people reach higher than they thought possible. What everyone looks for is leadership that lifts people up and helps them reach their full potential, not leadership using people as means to an end. Leaders who step on others for short-term or selfish gains do so at the expense of developing their people and long-term organizational achievement. So, why explore LGBTQ+ leader development? We believe LGBTQ+ journeys push people to become the type of leaders we want in our lives. Understanding how they develop leadership capacities, the pitfalls they experience along the way, and how everyone can support their journeys is crucial to helping all of us succeed.

You can't identify a leader by title or position alone. We can't assume a senior vice president of a major corporation is a leader, just as we can't assume a flight attendant or a driver for GrubHub isn't a leader. In his book *Leadership for the Twenty-First Century*, Joseph Rost defined leadership as "an influence relationship among leaders and followers who intend real changes that reflect their mutual purposes."[4] Leaders use influence to get things done. In fact, the Department of the Air Force's Women's Initiative Team, a fearless group spearheading major changes within the military fostering an inclusive environment, has a motto: GSD (politely— getting "stuff" done). The leaders you'll meet here, regardless of position or industry, embody both ideas. They work with, and on behalf of, others to make real changes and get it done.

We've drawn stories from over a hundred LGBTQ+ leaders with diverse backgrounds and experiences. From young professionals to senior executives, several nations, across businesses, academia, medicine, nonprofits, entertainment, and government service, these leaders represent myriad intersectional identities and perspectives within the broad LGBTQ+ community. We draw somewhat heavily from the military because of our backgrounds and because the development of leaders is a military imperative with many challenges and opportunities. We can learn much from what military LGBTQ+ leaders have faced, including the legacy of DADT and the ban on transgender military service that put a very visible "before and after" period in their leadership journeys.

We also draw from the military context an understanding of the environment and the necessary attributes of a leader. These attributes are not static, they change with circumstance. Leaders operate within a rapidly shifting environment that demands the capacity to thrive amidst continuous change. In 1986, the Army War College began describing the modern environment as vuca, which is volatile, uncertain, complex, and ambiguous.[5] More recently, the Congressional Future of Defense Task Force stated that "the changing nature of warfare dictates that the modern U.S. military will need an increasing number of service members capable of operating in a complex and fast-moving battlespace with limited communication or direction from higher authority," and that leaders and processes would need to be "more agile, creative, and less risk-averse."[6] These environmental demands are echoed across industries and sectors. Global influences, market fluctuations, and changing technology quickly and often unexpectedly force rapid adaptation or place an organization at risk of obsolescence. The vast amounts of data generated and available at all times can be ambiguous or contradictory and leaders are called upon to make sense of it all, incorporating multiple perspectives and responding to a variety of stakeholders. vuca language is a shared lexicon describing today's professional environments and experiences. Our world requires leaders to hold advanced skills and capacities to operate effectively, many of which are developed through the life experiences of lgbtq+ leaders.

Complex challenges require multiple perspectives, not just to understand, but to design and implement solutions. Diversity in an organization, when fostered by inclusion, is one of the ways to bring out the perspectives the situation requires. Fashion designer Michael Kors, a gay man, spoke about the advantage of having a different perspective in business. "That feeling of being *other* is often what makes you successful—because to be successful, in any field, you need to see things differently and find opportunities that most people don't see. You need to sense a good idea before it happens."[7] There is a rich repository of research that shows diversity helps create better solutions to the challenges we face, from creating business plans to healthcare outcomes, or in developing requirements for next-generation military systems.

Our contributors are an often missing, or deliberately hidden, piece of the diversity puzzle. While any volume claiming to have exhausted the list of possible queer identities can't possibly be right, we've tried to capture a broad and diverse set of perspectives and intersectional identities. Yet, if you peel away all the distinctive factors regarding their identity, circumstances, and work, you'll see one element clearly in each of their stories. They all want to make the world a better place. We want to show you how and why they do so while illuminating how they can go even further.

If you've made it this far and are still asking why it's worth learning about LGBTQ+ leadership, don't worry: this book is still for you! Everyone can draw lessons from the stories and concepts in this book. For example, we'll illustrate how transitions aren't just for transgender people. Everybody transitions! Perhaps you've transitioned from single to married or from one job to another. We all do it. The old adage that the only constant is change is especially apt. The lessons drawn from LGBTQ+ leaders and the changes they've been through have important implications for all of us. We thought we knew this topic pretty well from lived experience and education, yet even we were surprised at some of the things we learned and at how much more there is to understand. We hope the journey you're about to take provides some "aha!" moments that enable you to be more aware, to be a better leader, or simply to be amazed.

First, let's take a step into the past to understand how the environment around LGBTQ+ leaders has changed over the millennia and how the pace of change has recently accelerated.

CHAPTER 2

We've Always Been Here

On the muggy morning of June 18, 1983 the space shuttle *Challenger* rocketed toward space from the Florida coast. NASA archives list the mission as having two purposes: launch a communications satellite and put the first US woman in space.[1] What no one knew at the time was that the shuttle was also carrying the first LGBTQ+ person (that we know of!) into space. It wasn't publicly known that Dr. Sally Ride was gay until after her death in 2012 from pancreatic cancer. A press release from her company listed her survivors and included Tam O'Shaughnessy as her partner of 27 years, dating back to only two years after Ride's historic flight.

Ride was a pioneer in many ways. When you're out blazing a trail, scrutiny inevitably follows. In Sally's case it was for being a woman in an unexpected place, the astronaut corps. She endured questions we'd today call completely inappropriate, yet those questions based on stereotypes are still routinely asked of LGBTQ+ individuals in the 2020s. At her pre-launch press conference, Ride was asked how she reacts if there are problems or if she weeps if there are glitches on the shuttle. She quickly retorted, "Why doesn't anyone ask Rick [shuttle pilot Frederick Hauck] those questions?"[2]

Later on, Ride got a question about if she found the amount of press coverage surrounding her being the first US woman in space to be disproportionate. With an amazing amount of foresight, she answered, "I think that it's maybe too bad that our society isn't further along and that this is such a big deal." She continued, "it's time that people in this country realize that women can do any job that they want to do." She could just as easily have been speaking about her LGBTQ+ identity as she could have about being a woman.

Although she retired from NASA and divorced fellow astronaut Steven Hawley in 1987, and was already in a relationship with O'Shaughnessy, Ride was not public with her status as an LGBTQ+ woman. Those closest to her attributed it both to Ride's reserved nature and a desire to protect NASA. As of 2022, though one other astronaut came out after her retirement and another was outed, NASA has yet to select an openly LGBTQ+ person as an astronaut. In 2001 when she started her company, Sally Ride Science, with a goal to "promote equity and inclusion for all students, especially girls, in STEM," Sally and Tam retreated further into the closet.[3] O'Shaughnessey said they "just didn't think that Exxon Mobil, General Electric—you name it—Lockheed Martin, would sponsor us if they knew that two of the founders, especially Sally, that Sally and I were together."[4] They put making a difference in the lives of young girls ahead of their ability to live openly and authentically.

After her cancer diagnosis in 2011, Ride opened up a bit, but it wasn't until a conversation near her death when she gave permission to O'Shaughnessy to be public with her identity. Still, the instinct to be protective was at the forefront of O'Shaughnessy's mind. She recalled, "You wouldn't believe what Sally just told me. And what should I do? I want to protect Sally. I want to protect NASA."[5] Ride's obituary, written by O'Shaughnessy, was the first public revelation they had been in a relationship.

But times change. When Ride passed away, it had been barely a year since the DADT law had been repealed and marriage equality across the United States was only a few years away. In 2013 President Obama posthumously awarded Dr. Ride the Presidential Medal of Freedom and selected Dr. O'Shaughnessy to receive it in her honor. O'Shaughnessy's world had been flipped upside down. "What is going on in our world?" she asked in remembering the event.[6] "I wish Sally had been around to see all this stuff and to experience our authentic selves."[7] For too long those authentic selves have been hidden.

LGBTQ+ Leadership Visibility

So why are we seeing LGBTQ+ leaders explode onto the scene in the 21st century? We have a confluence of cultural change and more individuals identifying as LGBTQ+, so mere numbers could explain it. As recently as 2011, an estimate by the UCLA School of Law's Williams Institute said 3.8 percent of American adults identified as LGBT.[8] By the time the US Census first asked about sexuality and gender identity in 2020, data showed 8.0 percent of American adults were LGBTQ+.[9] A December 2021 report by the Human Rights Campaign aggregated government data to conclude "at least 20 million adults in the United States could be lesbian, gay, bisexual or transgender people."[10] Assuming the jump in the percentage of people identifying as LGBTQ+ in a decade can't be justified through population growth or shifting generational demographics, there must have been a shift in culture making millions of Americans feel comfortable reporting themselves to be LGBTQ+.

Are we hearing about LGBTQ+ leaders now because there are storytellers and historians who focus on LGBTQ+ individuals? Jennifer L. Dane, a queer non-binary CEO of a large advocacy organization, educated as a historian, believes what we're seeing is akin to previous periods where history begins to be explored. She likened it to the increase in women's studies beginning in the 1960s as women completed graduate school in much greater numbers and undertook the studies themselves. She believes now is "a pivotal time [to create] the archive of LGBTQ leaders," because we now have both the storytellers willing to capture it and people like her willing to share it.

LGBTQ+ leaders have always been around, and in much greater numbers than can be known. However, they're not present in Western public consciousness because they've been hidden by the suppression of their public identities, were unable to reach their full potential because of marginalizing laws and norms, or were simply erased through history being written by the dominant culture.

Norms of the Classical Era

If we go back far enough, LGBTQ+ leaders may have been more common, and perhaps even open about their identities. In the classical era of Western culture, mostly centered around the Mediterranean and fading out with the rise of Christianity, the dominant civilizations had a more expansive view of sexuality and relationships. Bisexuality was a large part of life in Ancient Greece, where "homosexual relationships were part of a life experience regulated by a series of social norms...and their alternation with heterosexual relationships."[11] We trace our use of the word "lesbian" to the romantic poetry of Sappho, a Greek from the seventh century BCE, and her home island of Lesbos. Greek art frequently depicts homosexual acts. Classical studies professor Victoria Wohl argues that pederastic (homosexual) relationships were "part of the sexual ideology of the [Greek] democracy as a whole."[12]

28

In this time period, across the civilizations of Egypt, Greece, and Rome, we find evidence of emperors, pharaohs, generals, and statesmen in same-sex relationships. Alexander the Great, a Macedonian king who built an empire stretching from Egypt to India, is widely considered to have been bisexual. Pharaoh Pepi II of Egypt was said to make "regular secret nocturnal visits to the home of General Sisene," which is assumed to be representative of his homosexuality.[13] Second-century Roman emperor Hadrian was married but many historians believe it was for show as his clear public attraction was to other men. The Museum of London says, "what made him stand out most amongst other emperors was the uniquely public show of adoration which he lavished upon one male lover—Antinous."[14] When Antinous drowned in the Nile, Hadrian flooded the empire with public art in his likeness, named a city after him, and dedicated shrines in his honor.

Concurrently during this era, the religious foundation of suppressing LGBTQ+ identities was formed. The book of Leviticus, written sometime in the sixth to fourth century BCE, considers homosexuality to be a grave crime. The widely used New Revised Standard Version: Anglicized Version of the bible translates Leviticus 20:13 as "If a man has sexual relations with a man as one does with a woman, both of them have done what is detestable. They are to be put to death; their blood will be on their own heads." In the latter days of the Western Roman Empire, following Emperor Constantine's official stance on tolerating Christianity in the empire in the year 313, these views spread widely in the Western world.

In a preserved text from 390, Roman Emperor Theodosius I decreed a rejection of what a modern reader would interpret as transgender identity and homosexuality. He said:

We cannot tolerate the city of Rome, mother of all virtues, being stained any longer by the contamination of male effeminacy... Your laudable experience will therefore punish among revenging flames, in the presence of the people, as required by the grossness of the crime, all those who have given themselves up to the infamy of condemning their manly body, transformed into a feminine one, to bear practices reserved for the other sex, which have nothing different from women...he who basely abandons his own sex cannot aspire to that of another without undergoing the supreme punishment.[15]

In Eva Cantarella's book *Bisexuality in the Ancient World*, she says, "there is no doubt at all as to the punishment described by Theodosius: death by fire."[16] Cantarella concludes her book with an examination of how morals changed over the course of the Roman Empire, attributing it to an evolving set of cultural norms where Christianity's overt condemnation of homosexuality found fertile ground. That confluence of factors led to nearly 1500 years in the West where LGBTQ+ identities were suppressed at best or led to jail or execution if discovered.

Driven into the Shadows

In *Homophobia: A History*, Byrne Fone details the fear and criminalization of homosexual behavior from the ancient world to the modern. As he puts it, it's a multi-dimensional survey of "the social and religious, legal and political, moral and philosophical" aspects of homophobia.[17] An array of persecutorial tactics were taken toward LGBTQ+ people in the Middle Ages and Renaissance, including a 13th-century papal inquisition to destroy the plague of sodomy, an Italian town offering rewards for denouncing homosexuals, and 1600 people prosecuted for sodomy during the Spanish Inquisition. In 18th-century Amsterdam, attempted sodomy resulted in a sentence ranging from two years to execution. Homosexuals were strangled or publicly drowned followed by eliminating the corpse through burning or disposal at sea.[18] Published in 2000, Fone finishes his look back by detailing how homophobia "stands as the last acceptable prejudice" in American life, though noting the tide was turning in the late 20th century, a trend which has certainly accelerated since then.[19]

Given LGBTQ+ persecution by church and state, the sparse historical record of LGBTQ+ leaders in the last 1500 years in the West is unsurprising. What can't be questioned is that LGBTQ+ people always existed; they are not a modern phenomenon. As we get closer to modern times, we see more queer leaders doing amazing things while suppressing or hiding their identities, and the cost they paid for doing so.

Freiderich Wilhelm Steuben, better known to Americans as Baron von Steuben, was a Prussian Army officer dismissed from service over allegations of homosexual relations. Though anonymous and never proven, the allegations prevented him from finding military work in Europe. Eventually, through a meeting with Benjamin Franklin in Paris, and Franklin's inflating of his résumé, Steuben found his way to America and offered to join the Continental Army with a promise to be paid only upon victory. In *Male-Male Intimacy in Early America*, William Benneman concludes there was ample evidence he was gay and documents the baron's relationships with his military aides as he transformed the army into a professional fighting force. Steuben went on to write the training manual for the US Army which remained in force for over 30 years. In his final correspondence as commander-in-chief, George Washington wrote to von Steuben in 1783:

I wish to make use of this last moment of my public life, to signify in the strongest terms my entire approbation of your conduct, and to express my sense of the obligations the public is under to you, for your faithful and meritorious services.[20]

Despite his success, von Steuben was granted only a tiny fraction of the compensation he expected from the US Congress following the war. Benneman posits that this short-changing was due to the compensation committee chair's "animus against von Steuben" due to allegations about his sexuality.[21]

Alan Turing, the father of modern computing, was a mathematician vital to Allied code-breaking during World War II. For his service he was awarded the title of Officer of the Most Excellent Order of the British Empire. Yet a few years later, in 1952, Turing pled guilty to six counts of committing acts of gross indecency with Arnold Murray, a man he had been involved with, and was sentenced to 12 months probation and "treatment" via chemical castration. Two years later, Turing died in a suspected suicide. Nothing about Turing had changed between WWII and his conviction; he was just as gay while considered a hero and a leader. He kept his identity hidden from most, even going so far as proposing to a fellow cryptanalyst, though the two never married. Turing was far ahead of his time, and only 41 at the time of his death; it's hard to imagine the accomplishments he may have achieved had he been able to live authentically.

In the latter half of the 20th century we see more examples of LGBTQ+ leadership being harnessed, but not highlighted. Leaders would hide their sexuality or stay as far from the spotlight as they could while still having an influence on the direction of an effort. Bayard Rustin, considered Martin Luther King Jr.'s hidden right hand, is a perfect example of this. Rustin, a gay man, was a brilliant organizer. In only a few months, he brought together 1963's March on Washington where Dr. King delivered his "I have a dream" speech. He also was a philosophical mentor to Dr. King on non-violence and a leader and activist in his own right from an early age. "Rustin showcased brilliant strategies and organization skills—areas where King, while a rousing speaker and a strong leader, wasn't as strong. So Rustin's sexual orientation was overlooked," for a time.[22]

Rustin faced the intersectional challenge of being both black and gay in the Jim Crow American South. In 1947 an experience on a bus where he refused to sit in the back sparked something in Rustin and he came out to his friends shortly afterwards. He recalled "The only way I could be a free, whole person was to face the shit."[23] Senator Strom Thurmond railed about him on the Senate floor to discredit the 1963 march on Washington, and FBI director J. Edgar Hoover spread rumors of a relationship between Rustin and Dr. King, causing King to temporarily remove Rustin from his orbit.[24] Described as having faded from the pantheon of civil rights luminaries, the producer of a 2003 documentary on Rustin expressed disappointment that so many people didn't know who he was given his accomplishments, stating, "It was his homosexuality that was always the rub."[25] In his last years Rustin began to speak out about gay rights and, like Sally Ride, was posthumously awarded a Presidential Medal of Freedom by President Obama in 2013.

Awarding those medals came amidst rapidly shifting perceptions and legal rights in the United States. The latter half of the 20th century saw governmental closets for LGBTQ+ individuals. An executive order from President Eisenhower in 1953 came amidst the "Lavender Scare" about the dangers homosexuals could do in the government. His order added "sexual perversion" to the list of items proving a federal employee to be untrustworthy, unable to hold a security clearance, and subject to dismissal.[26] His order was in place for decades. Its spiritual successor was DADT, a law passed in 1993 supposedly to allow lesbian, gay, and bisexual individuals to serve in the US military, but only in silence. Dixon Osburn's book *Mission Possible: The Story of Repealing Don't Ask Don't Tell*, bluntly said, "The law's goal was to get gays to shut up." Describing DADT as a powerful silencer and a federally imposed closet, Osburn's take was "gay Americans would be so ashamed of themselves that they would not be open and honest about who they are. They would not even speak up to defend themselves, to demand equality, to decry injustice, to highlight hypocrisy."[27]

Moving Forward

As attitudes continued to shift in the 21st century, progress and change accelerated. DADT was repealed in 2011 and other major federal barriers to LGBTQ+ inclusion fell shortly thereafter through judicial or legislative action. Two of the biggest changes were marriage equality in 2015 and transgender people being allowed to serve openly in the military in 2016. The latter was rolled back over the course of the Trump administration, only to be restored in 2021 by President Biden. The United States now swings wildly back and forth on LGBTQ+ inclusive policies. In the Supreme Court's 2022 decision to overturn the constitutional right to abortion, Justice Clarence Thomas went further. He believed the court has "a duty to correct the error" established in precedents like the one establishing the right for same-sex marriage.[28] The year 2023 has seen more anti-LGBTQ+ laws introduced in the States than ever before. Despite the uncertain direction for LGBTQ+ rights in the United States and much of the world, LGBTQ+ leaders are more visible than ever before, with several hundred LGBTQ+ leaders elected to public office in 2022's "rainbow wave."

So many LGBTQ+ leaders have emerged, starting in the late 1960s with the gay rights movement, accelerating through the AIDS crisis in the 1980s, and exploding in the 21st century. We encourage readers to learn more about luminaries like Harvey Milk, Barbara Gittings, Jim Obergefell, and Laverne Cox. Understanding that LGBTQ+ leaders have always been part of society, sometimes more hidden, feared, or demonized than others, is important to understanding the impacts of adversity, marginalization, and discrimination. What we see now as an explosion of prominent LGBTQ+ leaders, particularly in Western cultures, isn't an indicator there are more of them, just that they are more free to be themselves and reach for their full potential. Still, we're only starting to lower the waterline and reveal more of the iceberg of impactful LGBTQ+ leaders and their noteworthy journeys.

CHAPTER 3

LGBTQ+ Leadership Development

LGBTQ+ leadership journeys, particularly the navigation of adversity, create developmental dynamics that enhance capacities essential for leading effectively. The study of adult development informs us that enhanced capacity results from experiencing and working through disruptive challenges, and at times even traumatic or crucible events. "Crucible" is a word that originally referred to a heat-resistant container that withstands melting metal.[1] Here we use the term to illustrate the "heat" of an extremely challenging situation that tests someone to their core. The nature of challenges faced by LGBTQ+ leaders makes these experiences especially ripe to prompt substantial capacity development, thus enhancing leadership effectiveness and capacities such as thriving amidst continuous change, broadened scope and perspective, complexity of thinking, and leveraging diversity of thought and perspective. Perseverance and successful navigation of such experiences, even amidst the many negative impacts, enables these individuals to develop the leadership superpowers that perfectly align with today's leadership contexts.

Crucibles of Development

Illustrating how LGBTQ+ journeys through adversity enhance development of meaningful leadership capacities is crucial to understand why they are well suited for today's challenges. We explore the impact of LGBTQ+ experiences on leader growth through a theory of adult development known as vertical development. Vertical development is a transformative process of elevating a person's ability to make sense of their world in more affectively and cognitively sophisticated ways.[2] Cognitive maturation involves developing more complex and nuanced thinking, understanding, and sensemaking abilities. Affective maturation involves developing more emotional awareness and management, as well as improved coping abilities and resilience amidst adversity. Through this, individuals gain a broadened worldview, heightened awareness, and enhanced capacity for how they interpret and navigate complex situations.

Vertical development is contrasted with horizontal development, which involves competency building. Horizontal development experiences *inform* leaders, adding to their skills, knowledge, and expertise. Conversely, vertical development experiences *transform* leaders, expanding their mindset and capacity for how they experience and make sense of challenges. This allows leaders to process many inputs and variables, cope with ambiguity, and appropriately utilize and apply their tools and competencies to navigate complexity. In short, horizontal development builds competency, vertical development enhances capacity. Greater capacity provides more mental space for grappling with sticky challenges and unprecedented environments.

Vertical development occurs when disruptive events push the boundaries of existing thinking, enabling broader thinking. This broadening arises from disequilibrium upon recognizing the limits of the current way of thinking, prompting both the awareness and impetus to alter thinking.[3] Once aware of their current way of thinking, people can alter how they experience their own thoughts, views, values, beliefs, or ideas. When they've identified and acknowledged a certain idea, they may shift from being *subject to the idea* (controlled by it) to being able to *hold the idea* as object (or take an objective perspective on it). With this objective perspective, people can relate to, examine, and question the idea. Then they have the ability to control whether and how these ideas are utilized. This is referred to as a "subject-object shift."[4] Leadership author Ronni Hendel-Giller describes vertical development as shifting how people experience their own emotions, ideas, patterns, and systems. Navigating disruptive events and taking ideas "as object" enables evolution toward a more complex way of thinking, and thus enhanced cognitive capacity. Thinking this way matters, because "the world we live in is increasingly complex and we must evolve our capacity to understand, appreciate, and respond to complexity."[5]

All adults can experience vertical development, but it's not a given through aging. The more individuals are exposed to experiences pushing boundaries of their existing thinking and sensemaking, the more potential abounds for new ideas to stretch their limits and result in expansion—or vertical development. Quite often, crucible or even traumatic experiences are likely to cause this kind of developmental push—because the disruption in these events brings such discomfort and destabilization that individuals must find new ways to make sense of their experience and operate in their world in order to cope, recover, or respond effectively. In the struggle to navigate confusion, loss of clarity, or even pain, individuals might discover new ways of being in the world. While any difficult life circumstances can create developmental prompts, adversity faced by LGBTQ+ individuals is often of this disruptive nature. Not only can adversity, marginalization, and stigmatization create these circumstances, internally the very nature of wrestling with identity, coming out, or transitioning often requires a person to reframe and rebuild their own thinking and sensemaking. The journey of finding a new way of being in the world is exceptionally relevant and important to LGBTQ+ leaders.

Stages of Development

Vertical development evolves through increasingly sophisticated and complex stages of cognitive capacity. To understand the qualities exhibited by LGBTQ+ leaders, we draw upon developmental psychologist Robert Kegan's research on constructive developmental theory, known commonly as mental complexity theory. This theory asserts that our minds don't lose their capacity to grow in complexity during adulthood. Rather, adults operate from a series of evolving, increasingly complex stages (summarized in Table 3.1), allowing them to see more, and enabling them to meet increasingly complex environmental demands.

Early stages are less complex, having more narrow views and perspectives and fewer options for how to view the world. These stages crave stability and predictability and often exhibit a "one way to do things" mentality. Later stages are more complex, have broadened vantage points, and view the self as continually evolving or transforming. The cognitive capacities at these later stages are often referred to as *higher-order thinking*. There are five stages in this framework, presented as a continuum of evolving stages, where stages 3–5 (in order: socialized, self-authoring, and self-transforming) are generally defined as adult stages of development.

Vertical development prompts evolution toward later stages. Research shows that leaders exhibiting later-stage characteristics are better prepared for leading in complex contexts.[6] However, not all adults experience such development, and people experience different amounts at different times. Moving from one stage of mind to another is not a given; the majority of adults never move beyond the socialized stage.

Table 3.1 Stages of Mental Complexity (adapted from Kegan, 1994)[7]

Stage		Characteristics
Childhood	Impulsive	
	Self-sovereign	Self-focused; can only see own perspective; follows rules to avoid punishment or gain reward.
Adulthood	Socialized	Holds group viewpoint; values membership identity and harmony; team player, good citizen; internalizes institutional values; follows rules because it's "who we are."
	Self-authoring	Fully self-generated values, standards, and expectations; can appreciate multiple perspectives through lens of own perspective; clarity and perceived permanence of self and "how things work"; follows and promotes rules that align with own identity, values, and agenda.
	Self-transforming	Universality of thought; identifies themes, patterns, and trends across seemingly disparate information and ideas; engages in perspective-taking and issue-framing; comfort with ambiguity and paradox; sees and seeks many options and possibilities; desires constant evolution of the self.

Society itself, and most structures and organizations that allow us to function, are designed around socialized thinking. Predictable and manageable operations of our systems require rules, norms, standards, and people who willingly conform as they enact their role in the system. Therefore, most people are not significantly motivated or incentivized to move beyond the socialized stage—one that enables them to be responsible adults, good team players, and perpetuators of shared practices. Humans desire to fit in because our survival instincts tell us that belonging and acceptance into the pack will keep us safer, and we spend most of our time in systems that reward conformity and discourage or punish autonomy and difference.

Approximately 40 percent of adults at least partially move beyond the socialized stage. In this move, they go from being entirely subject to societal demands and reliant on external validation, to generating their own standards, and relying primarily on internal validation. At this self-authoring stage, adults "author their own book" by defining their own identity. This is noteworthy, because almost by definition, LGBTQ+ individuals, through coming out processes, have done this work to validate themselves. Only a tiny fraction (<8%) move past the self-authoring stage and partially toward the self-transforming stage where they see beyond their own perspective (with less than 1% becoming fully self-transforming). Leadership authors Anderson and Ackerman Anderson say leaders at these higher levels of complexity "see interdependencies that others miss, feel more confident in the face of unknown dilemmas, and can more effectively solve challenges that seem to possess irreconcilable differences and polarities."[8]

LGBTQ+ experiences being outside the majority culture can shift a person from the socialized mind to the self-authoring mind. What often drives movement from one stage to another, or at least the beginning of movement, is a crucible moment, which causes people to "see something that was formerly invisible," enabling them to change how they respond to what they now see.[9] Fassinger, Shullman, and Stevenson wrote about marginalization and how positive outcomes can emerge from those experiences. They argued that "learning to cope with the stresses related to marginalization actually may catalyze certain kinds of skill development that aid LGBT individuals in leadership roles."[10]

While facing environmental complexity or overcoming adversity can catalyze vertical development, more is required for true transformation to occur. To move beyond one form of mind, the individual must let go of deeply held views, values, beliefs, and assumptions of the prior stage. Further, the person must be able to operate within the uncertainty and discomfort of the highly destabilizing between-stage dynamics. Only by moving through this phase does an individual truly arrive at a more sophisticated, higher-order meaning system. So what dynamics are at play in LGBTQ+ experiences contributing to this kind of enhanced development?

How and Why LGBTQ+ Leadership Superpowers Develop

Vertical development theories help explain why LGBTQ+ experiences promote and accelerate leader development processes, particularly enhanced affective and cognitive capacity. Coping with adversity may drive skill development that aids LGBTQ+ individuals, not only in navigating their lives, but also in being more impactful leaders. For example:

> crisis competence developed during the coming out process
> may position sexual minority individuals to listen and respond

better to criticism; articulate their own points of view even in the face of opposition; create strong support systems; advocate for themselves and similar others within systems of power and privilege; examine their own needs, desires, and life goals; and take care of themselves psychologically, physically, and materially.[11]

LGBTQ+ individuals whose journey involves visible changes may experience unique impacts to leadership development, particularly relating to how they navigate and manage perceptions and expectations of others. Impression management and building "leadership presence" is something all leaders face and has implications for relationships, interpersonal communication, power, influence, and reputation. Added layers in this dynamic for LGBTQ+ leaders accelerate the imperative to thoughtfully navigate perception. For example, the new internal and external perspectives associated with adult transition experiences may enhance existing leadership competencies, develop new ones, or cause individuals to deeply explore the elements of self contributing to vertical development.

Cognitive Processes

All humans have natural cognitive processes in place to protect us from discomfort and pain. While LGBTQ+ people have the same processes, their journey may alter *how* they experience these things. Human brains rely on sophisticated protection systems and defense mechanisms to shelter us from discomfort. Physiological systems prime the pump in challenging situations by increasing the production or release of hormones like adrenaline, preparing us for mental or physical exertion required to protect us from threat—either real or perceived.[12] In fact, our subconscious often engages in avoidance of discomfort or potential discomfort without us even realizing these processes are occurring.

These protective mechanisms are activated by physical danger and mental distress, particularly from our social environments, such as loss, humiliation, rejection, or shame. We are hardwired to scan the environment for social threats and put up barriers to protect ourselves or to move away from social danger and toward reward. Neuroscientist David Rock describes these concepts as social domains that activate responses in our brains which drive how we react and respond. In particular, we are acutely aware of threats to our status, certainty, autonomy, relatedness and fairness (SCARF).[13] Our social contexts create multiple triggers for these anxieties. Individuals may perceive threats that are tricks of the mind arising from their own insecurity or misperception, or our threat response may be triggered by actual threats in difficult, unfair, or toxic working environments. Historically marginalized individuals still face barriers in society and workplaces and frequently encounter real threats to their SCARF factors.

Human cognitive instincts are so powerful that we experience heightened physical stress responses in reaction to social danger. Richard Sapolsky described how our hormonal processes mirror those we'd experience to help us escape physical danger, and the associated heightened stress response over the long term actually does our bodies damage, hence the prevalence of work-related chronic illness in our society.[14] Much of our professional identity is built around ensuring our "survival" by combating these threats. As such, the "self at work" is constructed around fortifying our defense mechanisms and strategically positioning ourselves to gain reward and avoid threat.[15] Impression management, social maneuvering, and socialization into organizational cultures are not just part of getting and keeping a job, they are mental processes designed to protect and comfort us—they are social survival.

Related to experiencing our social surroundings, our brain can develop an immunity to the discomfort and anxiety associated with behavioral change.[16] Changing, even when desired, means breaking out of the comfort zone our brain has deliberately created. Assumptions made about threats keep us captive to certain thought processes, and therefore behaviors, even when they are counterproductive to growth and self-improvement. Our instincts are telling us to play it safe even when other stimuli are telling us to break out of the box. Many people never identify or overcome these mental barriers to growth because it's so much easier to stay the same—stay "safe." For LGBTQ+ individuals, these natural instincts to preserve individual safety can be exacerbated by threats to physical safety.

LGBTQ+ individuals experiencing adverse or challenging situations may build different sets of responses to social stressors due to different demands for survival. To navigate their journey, they may have to address and overcome their natural defense mechanisms and immunities to change more quickly, or more wholly, than others. The process of counteracting stigma, fighting to establish identity, or safely coming out or transitioning forces the confronting of social anxieties and demands stepping out of comfort zones.

Therefore, LGBTQ+ individuals must overcome natural instincts for self-protection in a way not required of others. While LGBTQ+ individuals could choose to avoid challenges, those who deliberately addressed their identity may be more willing, able, or prepared to do the same in their leadership development. As such, taking on self-improvement challenges may become a modus operandi that loses a bit of the sting most people feel when facing change. LGBTQ+ individuals may tackle developmental challenges head on, more quickly, easily, or confidently than individuals who have less reason or motivation to endure change. Their experiences may make them more aware they're on a cognitive-developmental journey they can purposefully pursue. Bree points to a moment where she looked in the mirror and realized her cognitive growth would be stunted, she would be deliberately self-limiting, if she didn't transition. It was time for change.

Understanding how leaders develop, the pitfalls they experience, and how to support their journeys is crucial to enabling growth, leveraging potential, and empowering them. Ultimately, these stories help identify how leaders and organizations can empower, support, and leverage LGBTQ+ leadership superpowers for organizational success. Dr. Lorna Rodriguez, a gynecologic oncology surgeon, said:

> close to my heart as I have grown as a leader are those men and women who may not understand me well, but believed in my capabilities, gave me their unconditional trust, a pat on the back when I was down, and who went out of their way to help me move forward when I needed a push. Without that support...I think I would have drowned.

LGBTQ+ individuals thrive with the right support from their colleagues, especially proactive and comprehensive leadership that understands LGBTQ+ experiences.

Importantly, we want readers to understand how LGBTQ+ individuals develop leadership superpowers through crucible experiences. We don't want to trivialize these experiences by ignoring the damage that occurs, but we aim to celebrate the fortitude of these leaders, and help others understand how they can serve as allies and advocates. Organizational mechanisms and individual actions to remove overt and subtle barriers to LGBTQ+ success while empowering them to reach greater heights open the door to everyone reaching their full potential.

CHAPTER 4

LGBTQ+ Crucibles

LGBTQ+ leaders leverage opportunities to develop greater leadership capacity than might be expected amidst difficult circumstances. LGBTQ+ experiences catalyze journeys into leadership roles and enhance development of sophisticated skills. These include experiences related to protecting and sharing identity; navigating cultural, societal, and organizational norms and expectations; coming out; transition; and other crucibles, both big and small. These events can occur once, multiple times, or almost continuously, and often have to be considered for intersectionality, when more than one experience or identity is relevant.

Navigating each crucible can develop leadership qualities and provoke cognitive development. Further, the nature of LGBTQ+ communities and the way individuals experience entry into, membership identity, and relationships within these communities may also enhance development. Framing our claim about how these experiences enhance leadership capacity, we start with a story from Austin Wilson, a gay US Army officer. In Austin's story, he finds his voice after being pigeonholed as someone he wasn't. His challenges turned into opportunities to thrive.

My Story, by Austin Wilson

I am not a better leader simply because I am gay, but growing up in the closet allowed me to develop skills and competencies which improved my ability to influence others. A leader must demonstrate flexibility, intellect, and the ability to effectively communicate with many different people. The perspective afforded by my experience in the closet prepared me for precisely such responsibility. As I worked for years to conceal my sexuality, I learned how to quickly assess the character of others and adapt to changing social environments. By seeking to reconcile my religious and sexual identities, I practiced objectively examining arguments and finding common ground among seemingly irreconcilable positions. Most importantly, the process of coming out taught me the value of developing authentic relationships that can be used to build trust and inspire confidence. Cultivating these skills over time allowed me to develop enhanced emotional and social intuition, heightened analytical insight, and refined charisma, which contribute to my success as a leader.

Raised in Texas, I was steeped in the intricacies of living in a socially and religiously conservative environment. I knew all the sins to avoid if I wanted to walk through the pearly gates and, just as God created the heavens and the earth, Ronald Reagan was America's savior incarnate. My family, though full of love and good intentions, spared no chance to impart upon my brothers and me the importance of learning about traditionally masculine pursuits:

hunting, fishing, and football, to name a few. I, on the other hand, preferred intellectually superior activities such as choreographing dances to my favorite Hilary Duff album. From a young age I recognized I was not like other boys around me. Rather than sports, I threw myself into learning to play the cello. I took multiple roles in theatre productions around town. I found inspiration in the feats of Tolkien and Mozart rather than a general or a professional athlete. The more apparent such differences manifested themselves in my behavior, the more I received criticism from friends and family. Some days I talked the wrong way. Other times I was questioned about the way I walked. In one especially puzzling incident, a family member reprimanded me for smiling in a photograph. Apparently, even smiling the wrong way was unbecoming of a man. The older I became, the more I heard about the horrors of homosexuality and the abominations who propagated it. I often recall the words of a family member who, upon learning one of my friends was openly gay, warned me to be careful, because "sin splatters." People I knew and loved treated homosexuality as a disease that could be caught. The psychological hurdles faced by growing up in this environment cannot be overstated. During my most formative years, I was being taught that liking boys meant I somehow needed to be cured. If I wanted acceptance from my family, friends, and community, I needed to act the right way, talk the right way, and even love the right way. I found it curious: if being gay was so unnatural and sinful, why did a trusted family friend habitually approach me for sexual favors as a young teenager? Committing these acts of sin in secret only reinforced the idea my sexuality, and consequently my identity, had to remain hidden if I wished to lead a happy life.

Despite the ever-present fear of being exposed as gay, living in the closet allowed me to develop an increased level of social and emotional intelligence. Not wanting to out myself, I learned how to observe others, assess their character, and determine the appropriate tone, mannerisms, and vocabulary to use around them. From bible study to dorm room parties, every social situation required reconnaissance to determine how *me* I could be without the risk of others questioning my masculinity, and by extension, my sexuality. From minute verbal cues to veiled glances and gestures, I could quickly analyze personalities based on behavior and social interactions. I adjusted my own behavior based on my assessment of those around me to ensure I wouldn't reveal even a hint of my hidden identity. I remained cognizant of projecting the most appropriate image of myself for the given situation. As I became more involved in activities and organizations throughout the community, I gained valuable practice communicating with many types of people in manners that most resonated with their perspective. At the time, I had no idea how helpful this would become in my professional pursuits.

In my current capacity as an army officer, I foster the personal and professional development of the soldiers in my unit. I must account for the needs and goals of each service member and make a concerted effort to provide them with meaningful guidance and direction. Because the Army is such a diverse organization, my soldiers come from incredibly varied backgrounds. For some, the challenge of communicating with a diverse array of individuals can seem daunting. However, I can tap into the emotional and social intelligence I developed over years of living in the closet and interact with each of my soldiers in a more familiar and engaging fashion. Just as I used to assess the personalities of others to ensure I didn't reveal my sexuality, I now use the same skills to elicit the intentions and motivations of my soldiers. Consequently, I am better prepared to tailor my communication to each individual and provide relevant and genuine guidance. While my initial motivation for blending in with my surroundings was the fear of being outed, ultimately I gained the social and emotional competencies necessary to communicate effectively and easily relate to those around me.

Raised in a Southern Baptist household, I struggled to understand the feelings and urges I experienced as I came of age. I sought ways to reconcile my sexuality with the beliefs and convictions of my upbringing. Somehow, I had to decipher how to live happily in a world in which I was perpetually depicted as an abomination. I worked tirelessly to extract answers from different religious teachings, literary sources, contemporary experts, and everything in between. I searched high and low for any precedents that would allow me to hold on to the identity I wanted to claim for myself and which I felt compelled to present for others. I visualized countless scenarios in which I could explain my sexuality in a manner that diluted the hatred and misunderstanding of others. Surely there was a way to help them see the world, and me, in a more informed and empathetic light. I strived to compile sources and construct arguments supporting the validation of my identity in the context of my conservative social surroundings. In theory, I could one day use all this information to eloquently defend the revelation of my sexuality to my community. More practically, I attained a highly developed ability to place myself in uncomfortable situations, seek information from a variety of sources, and formulate arguments based on a wide breadth of research instead of my own opinions.

While changing hearts and minds is no simple task, looking back I realized my efforts weren't wasted. Individuals in leadership positions face challenges requiring them to think critically and produce creative solutions. They must continually draw from different sources, ideas, and perspectives in order to make sound decisions. In my quest to reconcile my faith and my sexuality, I gained valuable experience synthesizing information from various origins and carving out common ground among divergent points of view. Through research, I discovered countless examples in which blind obsession and willful obstinance formed the basis of a person's worldview and contributed to decisions that ultimately harmed many people. From these cases, I observed how inflamed passions can skew one's perception of reality. They impressed upon me the importance of making decisions based on evidence, reason, and objectivity—especially when in a position of trust and authority. I am a better leader today because I endeavored for years to approach complicated situations from different perspectives, recognizing that the best solution is not always found between a simple dichotomy of right or wrong. I am not afraid to leave my comfort zone and attempt to understand the world through an unfamiliar lens.

Upon graduating from university, I joined the Peace Corps in Ukraine. The experience promptly illustrated the value of authenticity and the ability to see the world from another's point of view. Learning a new language and functioning in a foreign culture demanded I dispose of my previous assumptions and place myself in the shoes of others. The war in Eastern Ukraine, for example, had no direct effect on my life. However, I came to view the conflict from the perspective of native Ukrainians and realized the war was as much an attack on the country as it was on every citizen's identity. The Ukrainians were shouting to the world that their destiny was their own, and that it was not determined by the judgments or expectations of its neighbors. I was inspired. I examined my own life through this lens of self-determination, and I realized I had been doing exactly what my Ukrainian friends were fighting so passionately to avoid. I had lived my entire life allowing my choices to be dictated by the assumptions and convictions of others. By staying in the closet, I surrendered any agency I had over my life to the whims of public opinion. I recognized I wasn't being honest with myself, and I resolved to stop allowing the judgments of others to determine my life's trajectory. Like my Ukrainian friends, I decided I would fight for the future

I wanted for myself. In 2018 I officially came out, though frankly speaking, to no one's surprise.

Coming out had a significant positive effect on my ability to lead. It instilled in me a sense of authenticity I had never experienced before. I felt more ownership over my choices, and therefore more pride in the work I produced because it reflected my full potential. As my self-confidence grew, I became increasingly tenacious when creating and pursuing my professional goals. I was no longer afraid to speak up and be noticed because I knew that ultimately the quality of my work would speak for itself. By ceasing to concern myself with the preconceptions of others, I could devote more effort to producing excellence in my work and depth in my relationships. As a leader, this tenacity translates to trust among my team because they see I am willing to do what is necessary to complete the task at hand. I found myself more thoroughly prepared to take the reins of a situation and be confident in the overall direction and outcome. Specifically in my role as an officer, the authenticity of my personality is crucial to forming open and inclusive channels of communication with my soldiers. When they see I am fully transparent about who I am, they recognize they can trust me to be honest with them when they approach me for guidance. By living openly, my unit sees that it can rely on me to be a genuine and determined member of the team.

Living in the closet was challenging and frustrating, but through adversity I gained valuable skills and experiences that continue to contribute to my success as a leader. Straddling different social groups and discerning the personalities of others allowed me to develop the emotional intelligence necessary to effectively communicate with different audiences. Years of seeking answers about my sexuality trained me to conduct thorough analysis of a topic and grasp the nuance of complicated issues without bias. Once I finally came out, I discovered new depths to the work I could produce and the relationships I could foment. By utilizing these abilities, I'm better prepared to understand, and therefore influence, those around me. I am a better leader not simply because I am gay, but because the conservative climate in which I grew up forced me to develop attributes that ultimately prepared me for the responsibilities of leadership.

How Individual Experiences Shape Development

Like many minority individuals, LGBTQ+ people face adversity, stigma, and marginalization throughout their lives. In Ilan Meyer's seminal work, he termed minority stress as "the excess stress to which individuals from stigmatized social categories are exposed as a result of their social, often a minority, position" and extensively documents the potential negative effects on mental health and development.[1] Yet, in a few areas he points to potential positive outcomes and benefits, particularly to individuals who find self-acceptance and affirming communities. That's where we show how those experiences can lead to positive outcomes and develop amazing leaders. In this chapter, we describe common crucible experiences and illustrate them with examples. That helps create a sense of understanding and empathy toward those facing these experiences and opens the door to the opportunities emerging from them. Lorena Soto, an immigration strategist and self-described queer brown person who looks like a woman, said, "Having to face these challenges and get consistently pushed down, at some point you get tired. When you've had enough you find your voice." As Lorena eloquently said, LGBTQ+ leaders find their voice, power, and purpose through experiences that push them down. Everyone faces adversity in their lives, but LGBTQ+ leaders often face it based on their identity. What formative experiences force so many LGBTQ+ individuals to protect their identity? As explored, societal views on LGBTQ+ people shifted dramatically over the millennia and are in a period of rapid change and backlash. Most LGBTQ+ adults today lived their formative years where their identities were viewed as something to be hidden or suppressed. If not, they might be shamed, rejected, feared, or physically attacked.

Transgender people face additional dangers. Beginning in the 1950s, they became viewed as tricksters, even by medical providers supposedly trying to help them. Sociologist Stef Shuster points out that "providers in the middle of the 20th century devoted a considerable amount of energy defining the moral character of their trans patients," which was turned into a method of discrediting trans people.[2] Hollywood provided an even bleaker view of trans existence. *Disclosure*, a documentary on trans and gender non-conforming representation on screen, thoroughly dissects the negative portrayals dominating Hollywood, from psychopaths, to murderers, to the ever-present trickster trope. A reviewer asked readers to "imagine how agonizing it can be for those who gaze upon the screen searching for something they can recognize, only to find unflattering, inaccurate and scornful representations staring back."[3] When society tells you all transgender people are monsters, it's hard not to internalize those feelings or repress your identity until it becomes too painful to do so.

"I felt embarrassed rather than proud when I finally told one of my bosses," said Fiona Dawson, "as though I had something to apologize for and be ashamed of. It was then upon me to undo those subconscious kinks in my own perception of myself and realize there's absolutely nothing wrong with who I am." Dawson, a bisexual woman, filmmaker, author, and podcast host, believes kicking away the internal sense of shame and embarrassment absorbed from the culture and people around them is a significant barrier for LGBTQ+ leaders.

Many raised in religious families or communities get their first impressions of LGBTQ+ people from their faith. Jennifer L. Dane's church leaders asked if she was gay. Despite denials, they attempted to send her to conversion therapy, a process attempting to convince individuals they aren't LGBTQ+ or at least to fake it. She described it as difficult to understand, marginalizing, and traumatic. Ross Murray's ostracization by his own traveling ministry team took him by surprise. He combined church life and his LGBTQ+ identity but didn't realize others might not accept his openness. He was kicked out of the group after four months, "I came out to them early on. I wanted to be very upfront and honest, and others had difficulty with that. [I was] being very professional and it's the fact of me being comfortable and not penitent that was an issue for others."

The church's use of "shame has completely enthralled and emasculated people in every way," said Reverend Cory Newell, a gay man. Shame takes away an individual's power, which is one reason coming out can be so empowering. As a teenager, when Lorena Soto realized she wasn't straight she was terrified and felt completely alone. She attributes her dread to her religious upbringing and family, yet she tried to pray it all away. Whan she was caught kissing a girl, her mother told her that would never be accepted in her house and that Lorena was sick and selfish. The generalized Western societal response to LGBTQ+ folks is an "othering," a view that stigmatizes them for being different instead of celebrating what having them around brings to the culture. As Brooklyn Marquis, a transgender woman and director of professional services at an infrastructure firm, prepared to come out, she did a lot of research. She said, "I tried to give myself the knowledge to overcome this guilt and shame created by society."

Coming out is a disruptive experience of defying societal expectations. That's also what keeps many in the closet, because of the risky step into the unknown required. Despite fear, coming out can be an opportunity to stop hiding, embrace self, and revel in the joy of being unfettered by constantly protecting identity. *New York Times* columnist and best-selling author Jennifer Finney Boylan seized her opportunity after a lifetime of identity protection. She said:

> A lot of your psychic energy goes into making sure other people don't perceive this thing in you, and that you don't perceive this thing in yourself, if you can avoid it.
>
> The funny thing is then you come out and everyone says, "That's impossible. I had no idea." And you're thinking, *You didn't see it because I spent* all *of my life making sure you didn't see it.*
>
> So, suddenly, I was free. There was some euphoria in being publicly female, but the glorious thing was not devoting every moment of my waking life to making sure people didn't know the truth about me.[4]

So what are the challenges LGBTQ+ leaders face on their developmental journeys?

Protecting Identity

"Our society's limited expectations of and assumptions about who people are and who they should be gives LGBTQ+ people two choices they must constantly make as they go about their daily business: They must either come out or live a lie," said Jeannie Gainsburg.[5] Before coming out, through attempts to blend in chameleonically, individuals conceal their true self while remaining in plain sight building self-management, interpersonal, and communication skills others may never develop.

When protecting identity, many LGBTQ+ individuals learn to "read the room" to get a quick understanding of the context. That teaches them to present themself deliberately and to tailor their communication style and message. Before coming out, reading a room is primarily a protective measure, but afterwards can be refocused as an effectiveness tool. When an LGBTQ+ person actively hides their identity, or suspects they have something to hide, even if they aren't sure what it is yet, they develop a sense of hypervigilance. They are acutely aware of their surroundings so as to not reveal themselves inadvertently in a potentially unsafe place. This stressful form of vigilance can be turned into a positive skill.

Tawnya Smith, a lesbian professor of music education, described the cost and the positives that came from protecting her identity. "Concealing my identity took a lot of energy I could have spent on excellence and achievement," said Smith. "That said, it also helped me to achieve a high level of self-discipline and the ability to be careful about what I say. If used for good, this can be incredibly helpful." For Jess Warren, a pansexual and non-binary leader in Facebook's Pride Employee Resource Group, the support of her colleagues once she came out was instrumental in her development:

> [My teammates] made room for me to be me, showed they valued me, and stood in validation and solidarity with me by acknowledging my identity. It enabled me to spend less energy hiding and more energy thriving and making an impact in my role. It was good for me and good for my company.

Navigating the Selves

Anyone is challenged when operating with layers of protection around their identity. David Collinson said that when people "divide their identity between the 'instrumental and indifferent me at work' and the 'real me' outside, they try to build a psychological wall between 'public' and 'private' selves, privileging the latter and [trying to] de-emphasize the former."[6] The public and private persona divide comes with the cost of people being unwilling to bring their full selves to work. The "self at work" is constructed around defense mechanisms and strategically positioning ourselves to gain reward and avoid threat. Many people develop discrete work selves and home selves to protect from the discomfort and exhaustion of navigating workplace social threats.

LGBTQ+ individuals may experience heightened versions of this dynamic across different contexts. Ross Murray described a process of "discernment"—the substantial time spent examining the many aspects of identity. He said these aspects are like a kaleidoscope, with many different pieces. "At certain times you twist the kaleidoscope and they all fall into place in a certain way. Then you get to a different context which twists the kaleidoscope again and they fall together in a different way." He describes considering "In this particular context, how do these different aspects fit together and what makes me *me*?"

Code-switching, the act of moving between intersectional identities and presenting a different version of oneself in varying contexts, is another experience many minorities go through with negative and positive aspects. "Code-switching can be a source of frustration, strain and burnout for minorities," writes identity coach Dhru Beeharilal. But when explored and mixed with authenticity, "people who engage in code-switching typically recognize that they get a benefit from this ability."[7] It's more than representing oneself with different language or mannerisms, it's seeing from different perspectives that can make code-switching a developmental experience. Code-switching develops the ability to translate from one set of contexts to another.

Self-Acceptance

Coming out is unique to sexual and gender minorities and is rich with developmental opportunities, many of which center around developing individual identity, says Dominic Longo, founder and managing director of the consulting company Flourishing Gays.[8] Coming out is not a single big event, but can be a lifelong discontinuous process. An essential first act is coming out to oneself and accepting the internal identity as valid. It may involve overcoming internalized shame based on stigma, external expectations regarding who an individual is, or normative sexual and gender expectations. Andrew Gelwicks said, "I internalized those dehumanizing beliefs about my sexual orientation. Those acrid, detracting beliefs others held were actually becoming who I was, and how I unconsciously thought about myself."[9] To overcome these beliefs, people need to reach a place of identity acceptance. In the words of Jeannine Gainsburg, this is when the person begins to:

> realize that they are not the only LGBTQ+ person in the world and they are going to be okay, will seek out others like themselves, make first attempts at coming out. How their first coming-out reveal is received may affect whether they move into identity pride, hang out in identity acceptance, or move back into identity tolerance.[10]

Overcoming these feelings is an emotional experience and a cognitive one. Because feelings have been internalized, often over years, individuals have become embedded within them, and altering them involves arduous mental labor. In doing so, the LGBTQ+ individual can overcome limiting assumptions and move forward. The journey is the emotional process of self-acceptance and the cognitive process of developing more sophisticated self-awareness, self-knowledge, and self-management skills.

Executive director of the National Center for Transgender Equality, Rodrigo Heng-Lehtinen's journey to self-acceptance hit all these marks:

> It took me a while to even come to the understanding that I was trans. A lot of transgender people know they are transgender from a really young age but that was not my experience. I did not have that kind of clarity or vocabulary. It was more like I just knew something was off. I knew something was different, but I didn't have a way of understanding why that was. The only way I could describe it was that it felt like there was some kind of fog between me and other people. There was some kind of disconnect. There was some kind of distance. I could never quite bridge the gap and didn't know why. It wasn't until

I met other transgender people—that was the light bulb moment, like "oh my God this is what's happening." So I did not really have a period of being closeted in the traditional sense. I had a long period of not understanding what was going on inside me. Then once I understood, I came out.

Coming Out

For many, coming out is key to their developmental journey toward the self-authoring mind. This is when a person "can define who they are—separate from how others see and judge them," and "can operate and lead from a vision of [themself], a sense of what is right, and a commitment to purpose."[11] Coming out was "bucking the influence and resisting the agenda that important others held for me," wrote Dominic Longo. "[It] continues to provide inner resources for authoring my own life story…the experience of coming out as someone other than straight has provided me fuel with which to resource my Self-Authoring Mind."[12]

Leading from a vision of self that rejects a societally imposed and assumed state of being is the essence of the coming out process. It's a refusal to be defined externally in who someone is supposed to love or who they are supposed to be. It's an authoritative declaration of authenticity and recognition that the only judge of that is yourself. Coming out provides paths to development stages most people never reach.

Coming out to others may occur immediately after self-acceptance or many years later. It happens with individuals, groups, or not at all depending on the circumstances, but regardless of how it's done, coming out builds leadership skills. With consequences ranging from loss of critical support all the way to loss of life, LGBTQ+ individuals put enormous mental energy into understanding their situation before acting. Even for those with no formal training, the coming out process builds skills in environmental scanning, perspective-taking, and risk management. Despite the risks, many LGBTQ+ people come out willingly because they recognize the benefits of authenticity and how it enables them to be their best selves. Coming out builds the dictionary definition of courage as the "mental or moral strength to venture, persevere, and withstand danger, fear, or difficulty."[13] Coming out illustrates the boldness of action in the face of uncertainty demanded of leaders.

Transition

Unique to transgender individuals, gender transition brings external perception and recognition of an individual's gender into congruence with their internal truth. Considering, deciding upon, and preparing for transition requires deep introspection and self-awareness and commitment to be true to oneself. Reaching an internal conclusion that an individual isn't yet their best self before transition is a leadership journey. It's a commitment to change on a fundamental level and can be seen as evidence of reaching the self-authoring mind, having fully developed one's own identity.

The ability to "let go" is incredibly challenging for most people and can hold them back, but people who transitioned have already navigated this challenge. "The inability to let go of concepts or processes that once worked, but due to changed circumstances no longer do, is all due to fear; fear of loss of control, of uncertainty, of failure, or of irrelevance," writes Dan Pupius, CEO of Range.[14] It's the fear some transgender people never get past, the fear that prevents reaching their potential. For those who transition, in letting go of their former perceived identity, they also let go of fear and move forward on a developmental journey.

Another transition-related quality prompting vertical development is holding multiple perspectives. Most people perceive the world through gendered lenses; perceptions of danger can vary wildly for a man or a woman about to walk through an unfamiliar dark alley. Few people have the experience of a trans person where their perception of the world switches from "How would a man look at this?" to "How would a woman?" Transgender people have engaged in both. David Collinson writes on the combination of reflection and multiple perspectives:

> We human beings have the capacity to reflect upon ourselves and to see ourselves as separate from the natural and social world around us. This sense of separation in turn facilitates our consciousness of time, our awareness of past processes and future possibilities. We thus have a capacity to envisage alternative realities and to re-construct and change our world. This creative potential enables us to reflect upon and exercise some discretion and control over our actions. It also enables us not only to "see" ourselves, but also to try to view ourselves as others may see us and to compare and contrast ourselves with others.[15]

Transgender people have layers of identity allowing them to relate to others' perspectives and vision. Taking multiple perspectives is critical to leadership. The highest levels of leadership involve "acknowledging and valuing other perspectives with the capacity to engage individuals and groups of diverse vantage points to work together toward a shared goal."[16]

Robert Kegan said the world changes around us faster than most of us can adapt, and the expectations on individuals "make demands on our minds, on how we know, on the complexity of our consciousness."[17] Transgender people place some of those demands on themselves, and the experience of transition points to opportunities where they begin to reach the self-authoring, and possibly even the self-transforming mind. In this state, people "let go of being quite so sure and see multiple possibilities and perspectives, many shades of gray," wrote Ronni Hendel-Giller.[18] Transgender people let go of many previously held conceptions, take on enhanced perspectives, and often see what was understood to be binary (sexuality and gender) as being along a continuum. Seeing things on a continuum, rather than black or white, right or wrong, is something a leader must be able to do. Though not guaranteed, the sum experiences of transgender individuals give them the potential to be truly transformational leaders.

Living Authentically

Before coming out, time and energy can be wasted as LGBTQ+ people conceal their authentic selves. Steven Yacovelli, the self-styled Gay Leadership Dude, said:

> The management of pronouns when talking about your partner or significant other, the dodging of "What did you do this weekend?" responses…it's exhausting! But that's the point on why "hidden" LGBTQ+ Leaders aren't as effective as those who are openly authentic and leading as their true selves: you don't have to worry about hiding your truth.[19]

Bringing a whole, authentic self to work frees up a tremendous amount of mental energy that can be leveraged as effective leadership.

Eliminating the impression management many people engage

in to cover potential weaknesses or areas of vulnerability is both freeing and enhancing. Authentic leaders put all their energy into the work itself. Further, these leaders have more to give, bolstered by the motivation to give back. Tammy Smith, a recently retired Army major general, said:

> My coming out occurred simultaneously with becoming a brigadier general. Being out made me a better leader because I stopped expending energy to hide and could also capitalize on the full and open support of my wife Tracey. She was no longer trying to support me as a military spouse while also trying to hide. I was finally free to focus my entire energy on the Army without being dragged down by hiding.

How Community Experiences Shape Development

Adult development scholars understand that continual evolution toward increasingly sophisticated cognitive and affective capacities requires appropriate blends of both challenge and support. The world provides challenges, the LGBTQ+ community provides support. Further, because much of adult development is a social process, a person's relationship to and experience of their social surroundings is a key facilitating factor. Our meaningful human connections, sense of harmony with important others, and sense of belongingness to the group—or member identity—all impact whether and how development occurs.

Developmental Communities

Communities built on values of openness, acceptance, freedom of self-expression, and the ability to continually evolve its own group identity are more likely to foster the growth and change of individual members. LGBTQ+ communities may provide fertile space for development and flourishing. "Intact sustaining communities have always found ways to recognize that persons grow and change, that this fate can be costly," said Robert Kegan. "If it is not to cost the community the very loss of its member, then the community itself must be capable of 're-cognition.' It must operate richly at many evolutionary levels, dedicating itself less to any evolutionary level than to the process itself."[20]

Many LGBTQ+ individuals find themselves removed from or ostracized by their earlier communities—perhaps cities of origin, religious groups, or families. Yet some eventually find highly supportive communities or social groups. In such groups, acceptance and ability to be seen also allows for growth in a variety of other aspects of self. Seeking out and entering into a community is a developmental activity. Finding new communities requires the bravery and fortitude to step outside comfort zones and open oneself to new experiences. Further, it requires reaching out to make connections, opening the self, and asking others to open to you.

Kegan described the immense importance of our connections:

The need to be seen, to be recognized, however it changes in the complexity of its form, may never change in its intensity... Meaning depends on someone who recognizes you. Not meaning, by definition, is utterly lonely. Well-fed, warm, and free of disease, you may still perish if you cannot "mean." Who comes into a person's life may be the single greatest factor of influence to what the life becomes. Who comes into a person's life is in part a matter of luck, in part a matter of one's power to recruit others, but in large part a matter of other people's ability to be recruited.[21]

Inclusion and Distinction

Another characteristic of communities that enable human growth and evolution is the space for differing, or even paradoxical aspects of the self. The very process of adult development—evolving from one stage of meaning-making to a larger, more complex stage—stems from two parallel internal motivators. Kegan describes this dynamic as our two great yearnings. "The two greatest yearnings of human life...may be the yearning for inclusion (to be welcomed in, next to, held, connected with, a part of) and the yearning for distinctness (to be autonomous, independent, to experience my own agency, the self-chosenness of my purposes)."[22] These two drivers, in their apparent oppositeness, may force us to become more complex to hold both realities, or to discover possibilities allowing us to fulfill both needs.

In the SCARF framework of social threats and rewards, autonomy and relatedness reflect these two drivers. They are how people relate to social surroundings and constantly scan their environment for either threats against, or rewards toward meeting these needs. Rock described the need for autonomy as a sense of control over events and a need for relatedness as how safe we feel with others.[23] While these concepts seem somewhat opposite, we nonetheless desire and search for opportunities to meet both needs. Certainly, a community valuing both, and structured in a way it could deliver both, would help members operate more effectively.

Might LGBTQ+ communities be inherently structured to provide opportunities to meet these yearnings simultaneously? Perhaps the imperative to create safe, welcoming spaces for marginalized people naturally fosters human connection and affords a sense of belonging to all who seek it. Further, the collective experiences of marginalization among members could encourage an enthusiastic embrace of inclusion. In these ways, entry into the community could provide an almost immediate, and maybe even unconditional, promise of acceptance.

That acceptance needs to ensure inclusion while allowing for distinctness of individuals. Communities designed to offer safe spaces and also to celebrate diversity, particularly through freedom of self-expression, allow members to experience the distinctness they yearn for. Healthy LGBTQ+ communities, or other supportive groups, encourage the independence and autonomy of being able to frame your own identity, live as your true self, and express self how you choose.

In most societies, the act of entering into the LGBTQ+ community is an expression of agency. For many, it takes an act of tremendous courage, perhaps defiance of another community's norms, or the risk of great personal loss or harm. Some take this step over and over, in new communities and with new people, meaning they regularly acknowledge their own yearnings for both inclusion and distinctness, navigate how to meet those desires, and take often-challenging steps to do so. These efforts grant access to the supportive environments they need to thrive and require them to undergo challenges and struggles that further strengthen and fortify the self. This exemplifies the iterative process of adult development.

Opportunities for New Thinking

The fear we experience around change prevents many adults from experiencing true development, especially where the process of change requires people to reframe or reorganize their thinking, beliefs, values, habits, or aspects of themselves that are deeply ingrained, long held, and intertwined with past experiences. These ideas might be experienced as the building blocks forming our identity or what we consider to be our foundational self. People are often wedded to or embedded in one single identity or set of ideas because it provides them the sense of stability, predictability, and control humans desire. People believe they know who they are, what they believe, how to behave, and how to successfully navigate their world.

Individuals are often committed to the aspects of their self-concept arising from ideas presented to them early in life, often from important others or membership groups. When change requires people to reconfigure how they understand or relate to their history, the immense fear of instability and lost identity is incredibly difficult to overcome. Author Adam Grant explains that "questioning ourselves makes the world more unpredictable. It requires us to admit that the facts may have changed, that what was once right may now be wrong."[24] In response to this discomfort, our propensity for self-protection often kicks in and prevents necessary or desired change and growth.

Personal change is especially challenging if moving beyond certain beliefs would mean no longer being a member of some important group. For example, a fairly common and painful experience for LGBTQ+ people is leaving their faith community because of the views their religion holds. Recent data suggest 46.7 percent of LGBTQ+ Americans identify as religious, 20 percent lower than among the general population.[25] This fear often holds people in place, stuck and unable to move forward. It can prevent individuals from becoming their true self or from taking the necessary steps to improve. Fear may also keep people from moving away from relationships no longer serving them well.

Might entry into thriving LGBTQ+ communities invite individuals to confront those fears earlier, more wholly, or more willingly, due to the need to reconcile ideas presented to them early in life with their adult reality? For example, if a child is told that a sexual orientation or gender identity is unacceptable, anathema to group values, or even that it doesn't exist, yet later in life has come to understand this as part of themself, how is this reconciled? There are both cognitive and emotional processes required to navigate these competing ideas and paradoxical understandings of self and community. These processes are required for an individual to reconcile ingrained assumptions or beliefs that at one time were taken as true, but at another point called into question.

Some ideas implanted in our minds while young we later find to be entirely false. Other ideas, once seeming like black-and-white principles, later have shades of gray. Still others may remain partially, or even mostly, true but require small adjustments to make sense or be useful in more complex contexts. All people experience renegotiation of old ideas into new ones, but the frequency we experience this mental struggle, the magnitude of the shifts, and our willingness and openness to the process all impact the extent to which we grow and change. Further, how intentional we are, how much value we see in deliberately engaging in this "rethinking," which Grant defines as learning to question our opinions and open other people's minds which can result in a certain wisdom in life, and how actively we seek out opportunities to examine ideas all factor into our propensity for growth.[26]

Perhaps LGBTQ+ journeys give people frequent opportunities to confront investigations into their own ideas, identities, and past mental models. The regular work of thinking about one's own thinking, referred to as metacognition, can result in enhanced skill and acknowledgement that the process is valuable, or simply less fear and anxiety blocking a person from engaging. These experiences may make LGBTQ+ leaders more likely or able to apply metacognition, rethinking, subject-object shifts, and overcoming limiting assumptions to a variety of experiences and challenges in their life and leadership.

Learning from Others

Beyond examination of one's own thinking, membership in thriving LGBTQ+ communities could reinforce this practice. When the individuals a person surrounds themselves with are also engaged in these mental processes, the overall higher tolerance for change creates a social surrounding that allows its members the space for rethinking and fosters development. Grant says that if people are constantly fed information and never given the opportunity to question it, they will never develop the tools for the rethinking that we need in life.[27]

Perhaps there is positive social contagion that occurs, further encouraging the re-examination of old ideas. LGBTQ+ communities might organically establish preferences for continually evolving the self as a community norm or expectation. Being overly set in one's ways would be strongly discouraged. Many members of the LGBTQ+ community have experienced the damage and distress caused by people or groups with stubborn mindsets, unwavering beliefs, or unyielding rules. The value around more agile thinking could foster a far different dynamic than most social groups, ones inherently structured around consistency, certainty, and self-perpetuation.

Facing and growing from trauma can fundamentally change how people know and express themselves, interact with others, and navigate the world. This theme arose in contributors' stories of becoming better leaders as a result of trauma, adversity, or marginalization. Many leaders acknowledge that who they've become is a result of the uphill battles they've faced.[28] Learning how others, especially those with shared experiences, thrive coming out of adversity can illuminate new paths in one's own journey.

In a thriving LGBTQ+ community, individuals can grow from their experiences of adversity and learn from those of others, especially where storytelling, mentoring, and supporting others' growth are practiced. "Inside our community there's this crossfeed where we inspire each other," said Professor Jackal Tanelorn, the host of Stealth: A Transmasculine Podcast. "I'm so glad part of me is validated through somebody else's experience because I think it's important to see yourself reflected." In this type of community the ability to connect with others is at a zenith, with powerful tools to forge bonds and share stories. With cultures of learning and sharing, individuals can even learn how to see opportunities for positive outcomes arising out of experiences they previously only viewed negatively. This community dynamic further enhances an individual's ability to manage emotions, choose reactions, and transform their experience of difficult events. Community membership, at its best, may encourage, enable, and even expect individuals to transform trauma into strength.

Learning from others may be a part of why many leaders have been so successful in their professional sectors and as leaders within the LGBTQ+ community. Many contributors described their work leading LGBTQ+ initiatives as stemming from desires to help others with similar challenges, a sense of responsibility to serve, the importance of being a role model, or a drive to progress society. They also spoke of the benefits they received from working in those spaces. They explored how some of their leadership qualities developed as a result of emulating the best LGBTQ+ leaders they'd seen.

The unique challenges and tensions around advocating for other LGBTQ+ people demand further development of enhanced skills. Leaders stretched themselves to be effective in responding to critics, weathering personal attacks, harassment, and cyber-bullying while maintaining constructive working relationships with people expressing direct opposition to LGBTQ+ ideals. While these experiences occur for leaders anywhere, the heightened stakes of being an LGBTQ+ leader working to address the immense opposition and obstacles to LGBTQ+ progress add developmental impetus.

At the same time, this dynamic also adds motivation to keep going, to continue fighting barriers despite the professional or personal risk. Further, the positive experiences of leading in this space fortify and energize them. Similarly, authors Isom, Daniels, and Savage highlighted how leaders of color can be advantaged by the experience of bringing their whole self to their leadership.[29] Their leadership assets and skills are enhanced from not only experiences of oppression or marginalization, but also the connection, meaning, and joy they draw from their cultures and communities. Many contributors expressed the inspiration, gratitude, and hope they experience in fighting for their community and framed their choice to do the work as essentially an existential imperative. They fight because they must...and develop enhanced leadership capacities because they must.

CHAPTER 5

Leadership Theory and Queer Application

Detailed in Chapter 3, the enhanced capacity afforded by vertical development is characterized by broadened scope and perspective, multiple lenses for nuanced understanding, mental flexibility, and improved cognitive processing.[1] Leaders with enhanced cognitive capacity are better able to recognize and address their own underlying assumptions, biases, or entrenched thinking habits that narrow their scope and limit their perceived available options for decision-making.[2] Leadership amidst complexity necessitates these highly sophisticated and complex thinking capabilities.[3] Operating effectively in VUCA environments requires knowledge and skills related to the context, and also enhanced cognitive capacity and broadened scope to make sense of environmental complexity and unprecedented constantly evolving demands. Modern leadership theories highlight the need for these capacities.

Studying leadership is dynamic; new theories come, go, and evolve frequently. We can't assert a single overarching theory of queer leadership to stand time's test. Rather, we highlight how LGBTQ+ developmental journeys serve as exemplars of two relevant modern theories of leadership, transformational leadership and authentic leadership. LGBTQ+ leaders' experiences prime them for success because they've already built the capabilities and capacities deemed essential by these theories.

Transformational Leadership

The discussion of crucibles in Chapter 4 indicated how LGBTQ+ leaders experience mindset transformation, expanding how they experience and make sense of complex environments or challenges. This expansion also prompts development of transformational leadership characteristics. Transformational leadership is one of the most commonly referenced modern leadership theories, with roots in the 1970s and development in the 1980s. The theory matured around the same time scholars began studying the VUCA environment and is often defined by comparison against a more traditional leadership model: transactional leadership. In a transactional paradigm, leaders hand out rewards or punishment based on performance. Bernard Bass, who led much of the early work on transformational leadership, labeled transactional leadership a "prescription for mediocrity" and perfect for leaders who followed the adage of "If it ain't broken, don't fix it."[4] Transactional leadership might work fine in a stable environment where repeatability is prized, but if utilized in a VUCA environment, corporations would fold and militaries would face defeat.

Transformational leadership fits rapidly changing environments. For leaders, it can "broaden and elevate the interests of their employees...generate awareness and acceptance of the purposes and mission of the group, and...stir their employees to look beyond their own self-interest for the good of the group."[5] Bass defined four characteristics of transformational leaders. They have *charisma* and look forward to provide purpose, pride, and trust. Their *inspiration* focuses teams and sets lofty goals. They also provide *intellectual stimulation* and *individualized consideration* to the people around them to enhance problem solving and develop each member of the team. These characteristics align closely to prevalent LGBTQ+ leadership capacities. This is because LGBTQ+ experiences contribute to development that enables transformational leadership.

Charisma

Coming out allows LGBTQ+ individuals to define themselves and lead from a vision of themself and their greater purpose. This enables them to provide others with vision and gain respect and trust through their own authenticity. Brooklyn Marquis describes what others see when they come to understand how resilient she has had to be:

> People that take a minute to think about what I've accomplished in this transition journey...they understand what adversity I've already tackled in my life, and the ability to live authentically, and not have any skeletons in my closet, and not have any fear... it commands respect, and it should...give me some credit, or some respect, for being courageous and brave.

Paula M. Neira, JD, MSN, RN, CEN, FAAN is a Navy veteran, a lawyer, and a nurse, and serves as the program director of LGBTQ+ Equity and Education at Johns Hopkins Medicine. She recognized that there is nothing shameful in being who you are, even amidst experiences of homophobia and transphobia:

> The journey of accepting who I am made that very clear for me as a leader. That's why I take an uncompromising approach to lead for folks in the community by being authentic in a public,

shared way. That's taking ownership, that's giving yourself a sense of power, and that's what I try to encourage people to do.

LGBTQ+ advocacy leaders provide vision and a sense of mission based in pride, trust, and respect. Tamara Adrian, a member of the Venezuelan National Assembly and the second transgender person ever elected to a national office in the Western hemisphere, described the work as:

> The philosophical concept of Ubuntu. It's the force of collaboration among people, respect, and the fight for human beings as a whole. I love and cherish this idea that everyone is able to contribute to the common good. No person is an island. Many years ago, before knowing the concept of Ubuntu, I understood it was necessary to organize the fight. To organize people, to create awareness, to create alliances with other movements, and to make people understand we have much more in common as human beings than things that divide us. In general, things that put us apart from each other are constructed by those who do not want people to become one.

Inspiration

Transformational leaders inspire, motivate, and encourage people, focusing on why they do what they do and why their organizations exist. Professor Amy Edmondson called this "the ability to make a genuine link between a task or job and a larger overarching purpose."[6] If leaders can tell the *story of why*, they'll likely be far more successful at inspiration, motivation, and getting their organizations to embrace change in the same way they do. Further, because of the adversity they've overcome, LGBTQ+ leaders often leverage their stories as inspirational examples to follow.

Division 1 women's basketball coach Becky Burke uses her social media as a public figure for change and empowerment:

> [People realize] "she's comfortable enough to post that. Here's the comments she's getting and they're positive, they're uplifting, and there's people that do love her." I hope people see that. I'm hoping that leading by example has been impactful and effective. I'm happy to be that person with this platform, and to help in any way I can for people to feel safer and more comfortable.

Blake Dremann, a transgender man and navy commander, described how claiming identity and coming out enables a person to focus on their important purpose:

> Our leadership is often forged in fear. We grow up so afraid of losing everything constantly. If I come out everything's going to go away. I lose my family, I lose my community, I don't know anyone else like me. Especially if you grew up religious. When you come out as gay or trans in a community of faith, you have condemned yourself to hell. That is the level that you are dealing with. You're saying, "I have made the conscious decision to condemn my own self to hell. I'm okay with that, and I'm going to rise up out of it."

The *story of why* that many LGBTQ+ leaders can tell has the potential to inspire others toward their own purpose.

Authentic leaders focus effort and express important purpose. Paula M. Neira said:

> Like everyone else in the queer community I'm living in a time of threat and fear. And that fear is not irrational. That's real and you have to accept that and then figure out how to deal

with it. My role as a leader is not to accommodate fear. That doesn't mean ignore it or be naive about it. But my job as a leader is to inspire courage. Because we're all afraid, but that can't be a strategy. That can't be the final word. This is what we're going to do to change it. This is what we're going to do to fight. This is what we're going to do to resist. This is what we're going to do to be resilient. We individually may fall but someone else is going to stand up and the fight's going to go on.

Transformational leaders inspire the next generation to carry the torch.

Intellectual Stimulation

Transformational leaders stimulate their followers intellectually by questioning assumptions, reframing problems, taking risks, and approaching old situations in new ways. When an organization's problems can't be solved by "applying existing knowhow and the organization's current problem-solving processes," Heifetz and Linsky call for adaptive change and a leader who can face the serious issues and sometimes "accept a solution that may require turning part or all of the organization upside down."[7]

Sint Maarten parliamentarian Melissa Gumbs, who founded a new political party in the country, exemplifies this approach. She described the seven-year journey in this way:

> We thought about what it would look like, what kind of candidates we would recruit who would be able to translate experience into policy development and legislation work that would improve the island as a whole. Caribbean politics can be very tribal—you vote as your family votes. To keep that vision of doing things differently we really had to break several molds

that have been in place for over five decades. We've focused on building a framework to train the next generation of leaders. We continue to generate thoughtful, intentional leaders who believe in inclusivity.

Transformational leaders encourage and stimulate *adaptability*, *flexibility*, and *openness* to new ideas. These capacities represent a persistent willingness to reinvent oneself and one's organization as externalities shift. Having reinvented themselves at least once in the eyes of the world by coming out, LGBTQ+ leaders leverage their willingness to change, even in the face of adversity.

In an ambiguous environment, outcomes are rarely certain and leaders must be willing to act on imperfect information. McKinsey business analysts say leaders "should rather act on what they do know, and adapt their strategy as new information becomes available."[8] Rational risk and opportunity management strategies require healthy doses of courage and boldness, particularly when consequences are high. LGBTQ+ leaders understand and practice risk management strategy and make decisions even when the outcome is uncertain. Coming out repeatedly is a constant instructor of good risk management. When done well, leaders are recognized not for what risks they mitigated but for their ability to see and seize opportunities.

Individualized Consideration

With individualized consideration, transformational leaders identify the needs of their followers and respond accordingly. This skill set aligns with another seminal leadership theory, situational leadership, developed in the 1960s and 1970s.[9] Leadership scholar Paul Hersey described situational leadership as being able to read a situation and identify the interplay between "the amount of direction a leader gives, the amount of socio-emotional support a leader provides, and the 'readiness' level that followers exhibit on a specific task, function, activity or objective that the leader is attempting to accomplish."[10] Situational leadership is about effectively adapting one's leadership techniques to the individuals. The key is understanding where people are at in their own journeys. Good leaders don't provide leadership to someone during their first month on the job in the same way they lead 20-year veterans. Understanding differences among followers and identifying where they are on their developmental journeys is where LGBTQ+ leaders shine. Their journeys to self-acceptance and coming out teach them the value of respect as a foundational leadership competency.

Tamara Adrian described how the trans experience in particular can enable a leader to provide individualized consideration:

> It's an uncommon privilege for a person to actually live in two genders. To see the world from two different perspectives, a very comprehensive view of the world. When you force yourself to see the world in a more comprehensive way [you become] a much more avid person.

Through adversity, LGBTQ+ leaders develop many characteristics of transformational leaders, and their experiences motivate them to lead in transformational ways.

Authentic Leadership

Ideas about authenticity in leadership have been around for a long time. People don't want to follow someone who is "fake" or hiding ulterior motives. People want to work with leaders who feel "real"; LGBTQ+ leaders appreciate this desire because they deeply understand the consequences of a lack of authenticity. Andrew Gelwicks, author of *The Queer Advantage*, attempted to emulate the football players in his high school. Of the experience, he said, "Much of my everyday mental and emotional energy was depleted, agonizing about how I was being perceived by others."[11] When leaders are authentic, they can put the energy previously dedicated to identity protection into building relationships and accomplishing objectives.

Examples were frequently noted by military personnel who served under DADT or the transgender ban. Kristian Johnsen, a transgender man and senior non-commissioned officer in the Air Force, said, "Once I came out, I put the energy I gained toward different things I was doing, whether it was professional development, being involved, personal development, or energy I could devote to others."

The 2003 book *Authentic Leadership* by Bill George, former Medtronic CEO, kicked off studies to learn if authentic leadership held rigor as a theory. While empirical research on authentic leadership shows mixed success, the popularity of this theory subsists in both scholarly and practitioner literature, and many principles George introduced appear in different forms across multiple works. Though George's book focused on building business value, he began by describing his beliefs about leadership, stating that it "begins and ends with authenticity. It's being yourself; being the person you were created to be."[12] He also described the dimensions associated with authentic leadership:

> Authentic leaders genuinely desire to serve others through their leadership. They are more interested in empowering the people they lead to make a difference than they are in power,

money, or prestige for themselves. They are as guided by qualities of the heart, by passion and compassion, as they are by
qualities of the mind.[13]

Characteristics of Authentic Leaders

Bill George believed there were five characteristics of authentic
leaders: they understood their purpose, practiced solid values,
led with heart, established connected relationships, and demon-
strated self-discipline.[14] In other words, authentic leaders know
and show what they care about, have no gap between what they
say and what they do, demonstrate compassion and empathy,
build bridges, and do it all consistently. LGBTQ+ leaders frequently
show this brand of leadership.

Understanding Their Purpose

Introspective LGBTQ+ journeys give leaders the opportunity to
think deeply about what they truly care about. Paula Neira described how the sacrifices and changes she needed to make to
live authentically enabled her to understand her purpose in new
ways. "My naval career ended when I finally accepted my gender
identity," said Neira:

> Needing to live as who I authentically am meant the sacrifice
> of my childhood dream. If we were having this conversation
> 20 years ago I would have described it as having to give up
> my calling. But hanging up my uniform merely put me on a
> different path of service. Discrimination led me into nursing,
> and then led me to law school, and then back to Washing-
> ton to work on the repeal of Don't Ask, Don't Tell, and then

subsequently changing the regulations that barred transgender folks from service. Today I say I sacrificed my naval career, but I didn't give up my calling. Because my calling was a higher one. It was service to country.

Practicing Solid Values

LGBTQ+ individuals are intentional about acting authentically. "One of the amazing shared experiences we have across our entire community is that at some point in your life you had to decide to live your authentic life," said HIV researcher Matthew Rose. He continued:

> There was a reason I lived a better life by telling people who I am. Authenticity matters, it changes perspectives of you, and sometimes those changes were not good. But people still make the decision that being authentically them matters. That spark of recognizing the importance of your authenticity is something we never put back in the closet, because we know what happens if you do.

Tamara Adrian's authenticity helped others embrace similar values:

> Once I was stopped in the street by a woman. She told me, "I wanted to thank you, you helped me to decide what to do with my life." The explanation she gave was, "I was in a very unhappy marriage for more than 20 years. I was even beaten in my marriage. I decided to divorce and now I have my own job. I am not rich, but I can support myself and I never thought it was possible to do." I understood that what we do is not

necessarily strictly for the LGBTI community, but for everyone. We become a symbol of freedom and a symbol of liberty.

Leading with Heart

Authentic leaders genuinely aim to do good for others. Professor Ed Hess says as we enter an age of massive disruption, it's embracing humility that allows leaders to "connect, relate, and emotionally engage with others [and to] work effectively in diverse teams and in environments characterised by volatility, complexity and uncertainty."[15] LGBTQ+ leaders often have an uncanny ability to connect with people. That connection creates psychological safety in the organization, which Edmondson says is "the belief that the environment is safe for interpersonal risk taking" and engenders a climate where people "feel free to contribute ideas, share information, and report mistakes."[16]

Matthew Rose highlighted how through authenticity, LGBTQ+ leaders care for others and transform lives:

> There's always a piece of us that wants us to be our most authentic self. Because we know the power it can have to transform our lives and the lives of people around us. As long as I am authentic and real about things we can disagree but at least we both know that we are truly trying to get somewhere. You know I'm being real about it and am engendering some trust.

"To really flourish, to go further in courage, joy and fabulosity, it lights the world on fire," said Dominic Longo on the role of love in the queer experience. "I call this the aliveness made possible by love. That's flourishing, loving ourselves, loving each other, opening ourselves to that ineffable love of the universe. That is the fundamental goodness that pulses through everything that's flourishing. It's our birthright. It's for everybody." Perhaps this access to love further enables the compassion for others exhibited by authentic leaders.

Establishing Connected Relationships

LGBTQ+ leaders are driven to connection. Notably, LGBTQ+ leaders' ability to take multiple perspectives allows them to appreciate others' struggles. "I love talking about code-switching because I dip in and out of it all the time," said Matthew Rose about how it enables him to connect:

> I became a really good listener. You can't code-switch without being able to listen to folks and being able to translate. I found concepts that are very universal. Sometimes you're talking about the same thing but you don't know the unique cues your community uses versus their community. You're trying to get to the same place but you can't quite connect. I end up being a connector.

Dominic Longo's journey enabled him to bridge cultures:

> I lived so successfully as a straight kid. The best little boy in the world was a straight little boy in my case. I danced the straight dance with ease and then I became able to dance the gay dance and bridge those two cultures. This became a superpower that felt natural to who I needed to be. It was who I had become, whether I wanted to or not. Today it's a valuable leadership capacity I see in myself.

Similarly, authentic leaders deeply understand human dynamics. Authors Anderson and Ackerman Anderson say, "The leadership breakthrough required is to see and understand human dynamics at a deeper level, and to master designing a transformational change process so it generates the best solutions and accounts for the natural human dynamics triggered by a march into an unknown reality."[17] The uncertainty and destabilization LGBTQ+ individuals have faced readies them to help others navigate turbulent environments.

Demonstrating Self-Discipline

LGBTQ+ leaders spend time observing, reflecting, becoming more self-aware, and developing a self-discipline through the introspective journey to claim their identity. Theorists Heifetz and Laurie refer to this as time on the balcony, where a leader pulls their perspective to observe from a higher point.[18] This is a critical capability for leaders to avoid getting lost in the minutiae of the day-to-day environment.

Dr. Russ Houser, a gay Army chief warrant officer, detailed the extensive self-work he took on as part of his journey, and the consistency it required:

> Being a leader had some big challenges. I had to break down a lot of self-imposed barriers that I'd been telling myself. I had to break down a lot of externally imposed garbage that I'd accepted. A progression of deliberate, forthright honesty and facing my own issues. That has really made me a much more effective leader. When you face something in yourself, it's so much easier to face things outside yourself. The act of self-acceptance is a daily act, and the act of self-love is a daily act. The act of growth is a daily act. All of those things are granular changes that we have to work through on a daily basis to make ourselves better. We don't see the results necessarily

overnight, and we don't see the results except in hindsight over a long period of time.

We don't claim that only LGBTQ+ leaders develop the capabilities and capacities to navigate VUCA environments, make decisions with alacrity, and inspire people to greater heights. Many people can and do develop into amazing leaders, whatever their background is. That said, the LGBTQ+ population is set apart through their crucible experiences and the profound soul-searching and reflection required to claim their identity.

Developing Leadership Superpowers

CHAPTER 6

A Sense of Self

We have explored vertical development catalyzation of cognitive processes that help individuals develop more sophisticated leadership capacities and showed how individual and community experiences of LGBTQ+ leaders may prompt, support, and even demand such development. Now, we illuminate how these development processes occur by exploring what happens within LGBTQ+ journeys that helps unlock these leadership superpowers.

Because most contributors are currently out, living and working authentically, we captured how they overcame adversity and how their experiences enabled their leadership. These stories show how essential it is that everyone should be able to live authentically. There is a cost imposed if organizations fail to recognize the dangers of not letting people reconcile their authentic self with their work persona. There's an immediate effect through reduced performance and a long-term effect in loss of talent and damage to people's wellbeing. Further, substantial positive impact is left on the table if LGBTQ+ individuals are not protected, supported, and enabled to bring their whole selves to their work.

The arduous journey of coming to define and author one's own life is exemplified in our contributors. For example, Brianna Titone, a Colorado state representative and transgender woman, shared how she deliberately communicated her authenticity to constituents. Honest communication helped earn trust and engender listening despite her hesitation about using her voice. Brianna's story illustrates many concepts this chapter explores as LGBTQ+ individuals find their true selves and develop as leaders.

I wasn't quite there [with my voice sounding like I wanted it to], when the opportunity to run for office came up. I had to decide, am I going to run for office now, despite this thing that really bothers me and is going to cause a whole bunch of issues? I didn't have time to finish the voice therapy I wanted to do. I decided, "You know what? I'm going to be myself. I'm going to be authentic. I'm going to focus on the things that are important to people. I'm not going to focus on me being a transgender person, because it's irrelevant and we're going to [campaign] that way."

The first time I did a speech in public was at the Democratic caucus. We were at the high school, with several hundred people gathered and I was handed the microphone. I had this speech basically memorized, because I didn't want to be reading off a piece of paper. I wanted to show people I was competent and I knew what I was talking about. I thought, "What I need to do is just get the stuff out of the way. The questions and all the things that people are going to be curious about."

My opening statement was "Hello, everybody. My name is Brianna Titone, I'm your candidate for House District 27. Let me first address the elephant in the room. I'm a trans person. Now that that's out of the way, let's talk about the elephant in this district and what we need to do to get rid of this guy." It was kind of a funny thing. It was a disarming thing. Because I knew in my mind that if I go up there and I talk about healthcare and

I talk about the environment and I talk about education, and I don't say, "Hey, I'm a trans person," then everyone's going to be like, "What's up with her voice? Is that a trans person?" I didn't want anybody just being distracted by that. I wanted them to focus on the message. I said, "Here it is. Might hit you in the head with it with a two-by-four. Now you've had a chance to digest that, let's move on to bigger and better things." As a trans person, I had to change a little bit of my style to try to get to the point and alleviate the fear or the question or the ambiguity of "Who is this person standing in front of me, and why is their voice not right?"

Often when talking to people at their front door, I didn't even say anything about "Hey, I'm a trans person. Let's talk about issues." I didn't do that. It was just about "Hey, how's it going? My name is Brianna. I'm running for House District 27. One of my biggest things is finding out what's important to you. What's important to you? What can I do for you?"

Sometimes I can see their wheels turning. I can detect what people's facial expressions look like when something's not adding up. But I focus on them and it's all about them. It's all about other people. Always about other people. In the role that I have as a state legislator, it is all about my constituents. It's not about me at all. Some leaders like to step on other people to lead and other people don't want to do that. In my district, I cannot afford to step on anybody. I won by [very little] the first time and I won by [very little] the second time. Every single person in my district is important to me. Every person who might vote for me is an important person to me. I think the authenticity I brought with my voice was enough for people to say, "I believe her. I believe that she's telling me the truth. I believe the empathy that I hear in her voice." Much as I hate that voice, my own voice. It's how you communicate to people. I've developed a lot of [authenticity] over many years, picking up on all those different things about how to get people to listen and to trust you.

You've probably watched, studied, and learned from leaders like Brianna. They come in all contexts and situations, from the coach of your third-grade soccer team to the four-star general leading thousands of troops. Like us, you're probably pretty quick to put those leaders in boxes labeled good and bad. Sometimes it takes longer to make judgments and other times our judgment is in error but we don't know it until a scandal breaks or we gain some deeper understanding. But what makes us put people in those boxes, and importantly, how do the people we put into the good leader box get there? How does their journey start and what makes LGBTQ+ leaders end up in the good box?

Good leaders start with a foundation of understanding themselves. This introspection builds traits commonly valued in leaders, such as self-awareness and confidence, as well as qualities that haven't always been valued, such as humility and vulnerability. It's also a journey that requires leaders to be honest with themselves. Without that internal honesty, creating external honesty, conveying authenticity, and engendering trust would be built upon a foundation of straw; sure to blow away during even the mildest of adversity.

A leader who knows their inner self still has a choice to make about if, when, how, and how much self shows to the world. When our internal sense of self matches what we project into the world, we call this authenticity. Authenticity is one of the key ingredients for leaders to reach their full potential. A Navy admiral described his career as spent wearing a bridge coat, a garment that protects its wearer from even the worst storms. Even though this admiral was a cisgender heterosexual white man, he protected who he was with this metaphorical cloak. Though he rose in rank, feeling its protection, the weight of it held him back. The effort to maintain the cloak became too much to bear. When he was promoted to vice-admiral, he finally cast the cloak aside. He let the people around him truly see him as his inner sense of self was laid bare. His happiness and team performance soared. For LGBTQ+ leaders, the cloak can be heavier and harder to discard. "I put on an exterior that I made impenetrable," said Michelle Macander. "I didn't like people to see my weaknesses. I was hiding for about half of my career." For LGBTQ+ leaders, shedding the cloak is a perfect metaphor for coming out. Getting there requires an act of confidence without arrogance, a recognition that their sense of self is secure and true, even while much of society believes otherwise or even holds them to be abominations. Coming out comes back again and again through LGBTQ+ narratives because it's not a single point in time. There may be some moments standing in our contributors' minds as bigger than others, but they have each come out many times. Kristian Johnsen said:

> Coming out, it's this event, right? But it's not. It's this ongoing process. It's every new group of people you meet. It's every time we [move], we come into a new shop, or we get a new supervisor, and those simple questions about, Oh, are you married? Yeah. Oh, well what does your wife do? Well, actually my husband... constantly having to do that.

Stanley Maszczak, a genderqueer equal opportunity advisor, sees it similarly, stating:

I feel like I have to keep "coming out" in the present continuous tense because the default assumption is everyone is straight and cisgender; meeting new people or moving to a new organization invariably involves coming out over and over again. This has different levels of labor depending on the person or group.

Every coming out provides an opportunity to build leadership capacities. Each instance reveals a bit of the individual's vulnerability in a way that lets others into the conversation, and can expand their circles of trust. It wasn't until her forties that Macander learned this lesson, but now she puts it into practice:

> I've learned I need to be a little bit more human to be a more effective leader. Be a little bit more vulnerable and open myself up and share some of the struggles that I've had to try to be more effective for those coming up behind me.

Coming out, particularly the first time, is an inherent act of self-authorship and cognitive development. Austin Wilson said his coming out decision was "a decision to transform years of self-doubt into self-empowerment." It's a move beyond societal standards to a place where individuals define themselves and their own standards. This capacity to self-generate expectations and goals gives a person a new starting place for further development. It's a path requiring confidence in an individual's identity and their ability to be authentic with that identity despite the shifting pressures around them to conform to societal norms. This journey begins with leaders coming to terms with themselves and evolves through developing an authentic and confident leadership style despite the barriers placed in front of them.

Searching the Soul—The First Step Is the Hardest

> Confronting our non-normative identities forces a level of
> self-awareness and reflection that provides a powerful lens
> through which to view the world, our companies, and our teams.
>
> *Sarah Brown, queer author*

Educators and coaches who help leaders advance their cognitive development begin by enabling people to identify and acknowledge limitations of their current thinking as impetus for change. Similarly, in the Alcoholics Anonymous 12 steps to recovery, as in other self-improvement programs, the first step involves self-honesty and admission that problems exist. It's often the hardest step of the road. For LGBTQ+ people, it's a similar first step. They often struggle to come to terms with feelings of being different compared to what's perceived as normal within society. The challenge compounds when the views of close friends and family, particularly parents, are unsupportive, often delaying a reckoning with identity. Wrestling with that feeling, and claiming an authoritative sense of self regarding sexual orientation or gender identity, can occur early in life or well into adulthood.

"From pursuing the most academically rigorous path possible, and to not just joining but leading various extracurricular organizations, I tried to distract everyone, including myself," wrote Jonathan Dromgoole. "I wanted to control the spotlight and show the world what I wanted everyone to see. I hid that I was struggling to come to terms with my sexuality in an environment that wasn't welcoming."[1] He held up his shield of obfuscation because he wasn't ready to grapple with identity.

Lorena Soto fought herself for years and tried to deny who she was. She had a raging internal battle over coming to terms with her identity and used alcohol to deal with the issue. She asked herself, "What was I? Am I gay? Am I a lesbian now? Well what does that mean about my feelings toward men? Is there a word for that?" She worried that if she was bisexual she wouldn't be gay enough for one crowd, or straight enough for the other. She often heard criticisms that she was greedy and wanted everything. It was very isolating and she felt very alone. She said, "I didn't know who to talk to, I didn't know what to do about it. I actually tried to pray it away."

Kris Moore knew something was different as a child because whenever he pictured himself sitting at a beach or going to a wedding he always saw himself there as a man. When he was young, he would write novels with himself as the main character, a boy named Kris. Despite his masculine feelings, it didn't make sense to young Kris. He thought coming out as a lesbian in college would resolve these issues, but his journey of self-discovery wasn't over. It wasn't until he came to terms with being transgender that who he was made sense.

Sabrina Bruce didn't come out until she'd established a fast-paced Air Force career. Joining at 22, she had already seen challenges in her life, some of them from feeling something was off about who she was. The military had long been a dream, but one she thought "was for manly men," and her enlistment would give her the opportunity to prove what a man she was without having to face her gender issues.[2] Things didn't work out how she hoped. Instead, she got the time and space needed to think about her gender identity. Asked how LGBTQ+ journeys heighten self-awareness, Sabrina said:

You're forced to take a look at your life and evaluate it. I enjoyed weightlifting before, and I continue to enjoy weightlifting, but I struggled with: does my previous self do this and do I do this now? Do I like this? Do I want to do this? Was I doing this just because I thought it was what was expected of me?

Sabrina's struggle is common through coming out experiences. People examine each aspect of themselves and ask whether it's who they really are, or what they've done because the people around them expected it. Concurrently, they have unique opportunities to closely examine each aspect of self and articulate "the real me." This deliberate exploration is an example of the subject-object shift described earlier. They've taken a specific element of their identity—something many of us take for granted (are subject to), and develop an objective perspective on it. Now they get to determine what to do with that element; they can truly own it.

This examination builds the heightened self-awareness important to effective leadership. In the words of Blake Dremann:

> There is a lot of inward focus before we come to terms with who we are, and what we're doing. That makes our self-awareness button a little bigger. We tend to be more self-aware of the words we say, how we affect people, and the encouragement we offer. We know how to talk to people because those are things that we pay attention to because of how people talked to us and how it made us feel.

Some people face the pressures of self-analysis as adults not from parents but from their partners. Savannah Hauk, a dual-gender website designer, said she "spent years on a rollercoaster of validation and invalidation at the hands of partners, which pushed me back into the proverbial closet." It took a lot of self-analysis and discovery to come to terms with her gender identity regardless of external validation. She described the experience as something that "shaped what I am willing to bear to be truthful to who I am."

Prior to transition, Brooklyn Marquis overcompensated for her lack of masculinity. She presented herself to the world as a "stereotypical mountain man with a Patagonia jacket and flannel shirt." She described it as crazy that she learned these behaviors and felt she contributed to a patriarchal society, even though it was all an act.

Human desire to fit in and be part of groups makes external judgments and expectations so challenging to overcome, a major factor in why less than half of adults move beyond the socialized mind. Getting past the group judgment barrier is often rooted in love. Fiona Dawson said:

> I concealed my identity in workplaces where I felt afraid of the judgment and stigma that could come from being out. The contrast helped me develop my own sense of self-awareness and realize working in that environment wasn't a way to love myself.

Cultivating a deep love of self was a necessary first step for Fiona that enabled her to better connect with others.

The Importance of Honesty and Trust

Having come to terms with themselves, the developmental journeys of LGBTQ+ individuals are just beginning, with significant processing of the lessons learned still to come. One of the most important lessons is understanding the value of honesty and trust in relationships, particularly in the workplace. Collinson argued that workplace insecurity, in "many different, sometimes overlapping forms [such as] existential, social, economic and/or psychological," causes people to construct workplace selves that don't reflect their authenticity in order to navigate the organization's social construction.[3] LGBTQ+ experiences within workplace social structures are often built on navigating insecurities. Attempting to adapt or reconcile their authentic selves with their workplace selves can drive growth opportunities.

Lorena Soto was overly critical and judgmental of others while struggling with her own identity. She felt her journey to honesty and forgiveness with herself led her to see people differently. Now, she says, "I never judge a person for where they are in their life. I don't have to tell lies to be worthy. In telling your story, you actually empower other people." Lorena rebounded in life after losing everything and being ashamed and humiliated about who she was. She shares her story because she didn't stay at that low point; she bounced off the honesty she found and now uses her journey to help others find their power.

Frequently, LGBTQ+ leader experiences teach them to leverage their own story in fostering honesty and trust. By being forthright about who they are, they engender reciprocal relationships with the people around them, leading to increased team performance. Equality advocate Taryn Wilson came out as transgender shortly before retiring as a Navy command master chief. Her leadership style changed when she brought her full self to the table; it enabled her to lead through adversity. "If you are honest and forthright with your folks they will return that honesty even when things are less than stellar," Wilson said. "That trust breaks down the us versus them attitude that can plague [organizations]. Being in a minority adds a layer of challenge...but once you [build trust], you change hearts and minds for the better and build a stronger team." Taryn's honesty with her team drove better performance and let her close her military career on a high note.

The reverse is also true: when a person hides who they are, through their own choice or not, team performance suffers right alongside the happiness of the leader. Sybil Taunton, a communications director and Air Force veteran, obfuscated herself while serving as revealing her sexuality could have ended her career:

> Serving under DADT was the ultimate moral dilemma for me. Honesty and transparency are really important values, and being forced to lead without being able to fully commit to those values was incredibly difficult. I'm not one for sharing loads about my personal life, but having to lie when asked questions by people I led who wanted to know more about who I am and where I came from felt awful. After repeal, I made it my priority to ensure every airman I led had the safe space to feel a part of the team and to be who they were without ever feeling like they had to lie or hide the people they love. Effective collaboration, team building and overall mission success all rely on trust, and in order to trust each other we need to know each other and the wonderful things that make us who we are.

Sabrina Bruce had similar experiences learning the value of trust and honesty as the bedrock of leadership following her transition.

> Without honesty, a leader is hollow. My first three years in the military I wasn't honest with myself. My relationships suffered, I argued with coworkers over perceived slights of my masculinity, I tried to prove myself by being cocky and arrogant. None of it worked.

> Only when I was honest with myself did I begin to shine as a leader because you can only carry the charade so far. Yes, you may succeed fooling the world for a while, but I never was able to fool myself. Doubt gnawed at everything I did. All

my success was tainted as my mind betrayed me, constantly reminding me that if any coworkers or supervisors truly knew who I was, they would take everything from me.

This proved to me that if you can only be one thing in life, you have to be honest. Honest with yourself, honest with family, honest with your boss, everyone. Without honesty, your foundation will always feel shaky, because it will be built on false pretenses.

Building a foundation for future growth is what LGBTQ+ leaders do when they begin with honesty about themselves. Russell Houser's commitment to honesty began when he finally understood his sexuality. It's what allows him to now focus on his work of teaching and mentoring. When people lie to others, there's an energy cost to maintain those lies, and the same is true when they lie to themselves about who they are. Kegan and Lahey pointed out the problem of wasted energy within workplaces as an unpaid second job: "Most people are spending time and energy covering up their weaknesses, managing other people's impressions of them, showing themselves to their best advantage, playing politics, hiding their inadequacies, hiding their uncertainties, hiding their limitations. Hiding."[4] They explain how this wasted energy is a huge loss of resources to an organization and prevents people from reaching their full potential.

Is Being Openly LGBTQ+ a Vulnerability?

Vulnerability is often viewed as something to avoid at all costs. Until recently, describing vulnerability as a leadership trait might get a person laughed out of a room. Thinkers like Dr. Brené Brown recently popularized a reframing of vulnerability. Vulnerability definitions break into two parts; the first is openness and the second is exposure to potential sources of harm. Sadly, this remains true for many openly LGBTQ+ individuals. Their rights, emotions, and bodies are often attacked based on their openness.

From a leadership perspective, there is a different way to wield vulnerability. Being open and exposed doesn't only create avenues of potential attack, it creates pathways to connection and relationship building. Michelle Macander said that people "expect leaders to be competent but they also expect them to be human. When people see you struggle but overcome things, they're going to respond to you and you're going to get a lot more out of them." She believes the connection grown out of vulnerability and shared humanity drives her folks to higher performance. Film and television writer, director, and producer Scottie Jeanette Madden said:

> Vulnerability is one of the feminine virtues that I couldn't wait to really dive into. I was taught that it was a weakness. I was socialized as a boy. And not everything I was taught was right. Vulnerability is where the empathy kicks in and I'm showing you just how secure I am. I'm not a dog lying on the ground showing you my belly, I'm a woman standing up showing you my heart. Don't think that you can come in and break it. But it's still right here.

LGBTQ+ leaders have done the math, often repeatedly, and decide the risks of harm, of their heart getting broken, are less than the benefits accrued from connections forged through vulnerability. When people open themselves up, they let others in. Projecting an impenetrable suit of armor may protect individuals, but that also isolates them. Jennifer L. Dane is incredibly open about her vulnerabilities, having learnt that it rarely worked in her favor to hide them. Two weeks before our conversation, Jennifer attempted suicide due to her struggles with self-doubt. In revealing that to others she sought and found connections that enabled her to get help and continue her mission to help others. Bonds formed through vulnerability, showing humanity and a willingness to accept others as such, pay dividends well beyond the threats of harm that may occur.

Coast Guard commander Amanda Fisher calculated the risk and was pleasantly surprised to be right; the benefits of her openness far exceeded the cost. People told Amanda on multiple occasions they felt she was trustworthy because her transition exhibited honesty, vulnerability, and a sense of integrity they found refreshing. Her takeaway was "the lesson for any leader is that showing honesty by professionally and appropriately revealing a personal vulnerability can go a long way in building trust with the people you lead."

Being vulnerable and building connections often starts chain reactions that vastly multiply the power of one individual opening up. "It's about putting yourself out there, letting people know who you are, and opening yourself up," said Kristian Johnsen:

> It goes back to trust. When you see somebody put themself out there, it makes you want to do the same thing. The more we're authentic, vulnerable, and bring our walls down, it enables us to be a better team. The only way we get anything done is through teamwork and trust. We don't have to agree all the time or all think the same. In fact, it's better if we don't, but if we're vulnerable with each other we feel we can put our ideas out there and be heard. We can come together to make the best decision with different inputs and different voices, and people feeling respected and heard.

Kristian also said, "authentic and vulnerable leaders are an absolute necessity." He listened to senior leaders discuss challenges they had overcome and learned from the vulnerability they displayed. It was okay not to be okay, reaching out for help is valuable, and you can still be successful even when you ask for help or work through mental health issues.

Air Force lieutenant colonel Julie Janson also experienced the multiplying effect of vulnerability. Julie served a portion of her career unable to be open about her identity. She suffered as an individual and as a leader until she was able to open up about herself.

> The more I embrace my divine femininity, queerness, and uniqueness, the happier I am. I've stopped trying to blend in, and have embraced standing out. This is so much easier than pretending to be someone I'm not, because it turns out people find you much more approachable when you're vulnerable, and like you more when you're authentic. I do better work and have deeper relationships since embracing who I am. I tell people I love them all the time and even if it completely freaks them out at first, the number of people reaching out to me grows and grows.

In an article about her lessons learned while in command, Bree described how she felt vulnerability led to opportunity. Bree had been perceived as relatively arrogant and unapproachable prior to her coming out. She said:

> Opening up about who I am as a transgender person created the space for trust. Not the kind of trust coming from knowing the person next to you will accomplish the mission, but the kind of trust where people put their faith in you to help them through difficult times. More than once, I heard some variation of "If I didn't know your story, I wouldn't be sharing this..."[5]

Vulnerability is not all about weakness, it's an opening that lets people connect and build together.

The Downside of Inauthenticity

Authenticity came up *often* from contributors and was valued highly in their leadership toolbox. "Authenticity is the root of how I lead," said Jennifer L. Dane. Alternatively, negative experiences can occur when people can't be authentic. Alexandria Holder spent most of her career closeted. "So much time and energy was spent on hiding that I couldn't devote myself fully to my job, my service to my country, or to my friends and family," said Holder. "I was, in many ways, a partial person, only able to apply 75 percent of myself and using the other 25 percent keeping myself from losing my job, friends, or family."

Developmental experts Kegan *et al.* (2014) have shown that:

> most people at work, even in high-performing organizations, divert considerable energy every day to a second job that no one has hired them to do: preserving their reputation, putting their best selves forward, and hiding their inadequacies from others and themselves. We believe this is the single biggest cause of wasted resources in nearly every company today.[6]

Their research highlights the pitfalls of lack of authenticity. Post-coming out, Pfizer executive vice president Sally Susman saw how limited she'd been before living authentically, which she described as "playing with my whole heart and speaking with my full throat." As a communicator, that was everything to her. She went on to say, "when someone is closeted, they become a very inauthentic messenger. I found that by coming out, I was practicing what I was preaching through everyone I was advising, to say, 'You need to be fully forthcoming.' I felt that gave me a lot of power."[7] Closeted inauthenticity in communication drives a lack of trust and significantly hinders leadership effectiveness.

Kristian Johnsen was closeted for much of their time in service. "There came a point where my coworkers stopped inviting me to things because I said 'no' so many times to protect my personal life and any questions that might come up about it," said Johnsen. They missed out on developing the connections that make an organization thrive. However, once they came out, the situation changed. They now describe their network as "the best relationships" and "an ability to share deeper personal stories," which creates room for growth and organizational success.

Michelle Macander described introducing her wife at a military ball and no longer keeping secrets as liberating. "You're a more effective leader because you have more confidence in yourself," said Macander. "There isn't an internal struggle you're fighting with that takes a lot of energy away from doing what you have to do." She described how her life would have been different if she had continued diverting energy into hiding:

> I would have missed out. If I was still in a relationship with my wife but she wasn't a part of my military life, I wouldn't have been going to a lot of events. My life would've been completely bifurcated. I would be that Marine that clocks out at 5:00 and goes home and never the two should meet. That makes for a less effective Marine because it's not a 9:00 to 5:00 job. It's a calling. If I had to keep those things completely separate then it would've caused serious problems with my marriage and it would've caused serious problems with my career because I wouldn't be able to focus on it when I had to. They always would be in conflict. Instead the Marines understand when I'm

at home they're not going to bother me unless it's something important. And my wife understands if they do contact me it's because it is necessary. It would've been impossible for me to be where I am today if that had been the case.

Lindsey Medina, an Air Force officer, knew she was gay when she was eight and developed a crush on her best friend there was no denying. However, she was in a Catholic school and would be all through high school.

My parents were really Catholic, my family's really Catholic. So, I told myself [being gay] is a part of me I need to put away. A part of me I can't express. So how do I come across as authentic and genuine and get to know people and connect to people without the part of me I'd like to share?

I had to figure it out. I don't think people understood how discriminatory they were at school, because I wasn't out. If nobody's out and LGBTQ in the school then people say a lot of wild things you can't check them for because then they'd ask, "Oh, well, are you?"

I had to agree to disagree. I had to put that aside and see where I could connect with them. Maybe if I was out they wouldn't want to talk with me or they wouldn't want me to be on their softball team, but where can we connect? We're both big sisters, or we both like to read and write. I looked for ways I could connect with people or help them in order for them to not think of me as LGBTQ.

My goal was always to get people to think of me as something else, so when I eventually came out, I wouldn't lose my entire network of people, my entire community. That's a messed up way for a kid to think. I've been thinking that way since I was a little kid. My goal going into any situation, such as a new team, class, or environment, was, how can I win them over, so when I come out of the closet, they're still able to see me and not the big rainbow pride flag that people tend to tack over your face.

Even in the negative example of what happens when a person can't be authentic, we see skill building. Lindsey's experiences taught her how to find a connection with others despite differences, which is incredibly useful in many contexts. Similarly, Sybill Taunton said:

I had to adapt and figure out how to earn people's trust and confidence while being cryptic and keeping a major part of myself hidden. I had to learn how to choose my words carefully and be as much of myself as I could be without exposing myself, analyzing people and behaviors to know who I could trust and who I couldn't, like a self-aware sociopath.

Though Lindsey and Sybill used connection building to protect themselves, that same skill set plays into many aspects of leadership, including team building, negotiations, finding common ground despite differences, and being an ally or advocate for others.

The Confidence of Authentic Leadership

Once living authentically, LGBTQ+ leaders understand how to garner the trust that builds and maintains relationships. They're also willing to connect with others through their vulnerability. These leaders moved beyond the socialized mind and claimed self-authorship over their lives. By proclaiming who they are, they've confidently defined their identity and set standards for themselves.

Lorena Soto spent a lot of energy protecting her identity, but when it became too much to endure, she came out despite her fears. She felt leaders needed to be honest and it felt wrong for her to be dishonest about herself. "In facing this struggle of figuring it out, you have to develop genuine courage and strength," said Soto. "You have to know how to pull yourself up." There is often a sense of confidence and relief that accompanies coming out. Lorena believes confidence and courage are forged through negative and challenging experiences:

> I hate that [LGBTQ+ people] have to go through those experiences, but the courage for them to be who they are is beautiful, it's courageous. I think that's what makes us leaders. We go through the internal struggle of facing the world, deciding am I going to hide or am I going to be who I am despite what everybody else thinks.

Getting to that point takes a lot. Division 1 women's basketball coach Becky Burke spoke about that struggle:

> It's scary to think you have something that if you put it out there people won't like you for it, and people won't love you for it, and people will have something negative to say. You are afraid of seeing something you don't want to see or hearing something from your parents that you don't want to hear. You've got to be prepared for that. You've got to be ready. Ultimately wanting to live your authentic self has to be greater than the fear of what might be said. That's a hard point to get to, it really is.

Unique to coming out in the military is facing dissonance between being closeted and the service core values such as integrity and honesty. Reconciling those stressors through coming out builds the character the military demands. Satellite communications operations manager Kimberly Morris, a retired Marine Corps major, said before transitioning, she was "so scared of failure and afraid of having to confront my true self that I kept plodding on [in the closet]." Now that she's resolved the conflict between service values and identity she's driven forward "with positive energy and not fear." Her confidence soared as her fear evaporated:

> I was no longer spending time and energy trying to edit myself to conform. I carried a mild case of depression mixed with anxiety prior to transition because I never felt aligned, and since I couldn't "fix" myself it eroded my confidence. Little issues became huge issues. Once I transitioned, issues with self started to fall away.

Michelle Macander found a weight lifted from her shoulders after coming out:

> It was liberating to not have it be a secret. That makes you a more effective leader because you have a lot more confidence in yourself. There isn't an internal struggle that you're fighting with that takes a lot of energy away from doing what you have to do.

With the following story, consider this chapter's arc. Harry Walter, a transgender major in the British Army, embraces a transformational journey to lead with confidence, leverage his experience, and improve the lives of those around him. Harry also foreshadows later topics regarding how colleagues and bosses helped create the environment for his success.

My Story, by Harry Walter

When I entered military service, I was a woman. I served as a female officer for the first four years of my service, transitioned in my late 20s, and am now living comfortably and happily as a man.

Coming out for the first time was not an easy or comfortable process. I always felt uncomfortable with a female body and identity. When I was a small child, long before I knew the word "transgender," I knew I wanted to be a boy. Learning, first, the vocabulary to articulate what I felt, and much later, the confidence to express that to anyone else, took until I was in my mid-20s. When the time came, I was fortunate to be working in a stable job, based in my home country, with a chain of command that I trusted and a supportive family environment.

After a good deal of soul-searching, I did what any responsible young officer does when something big is happening in their personal life; I booked an appointment in my commander's diary and asked to speak with her privately. I rehearsed over and over in my head what I was going to say. At the appointed hour, I walked in, shut the door, took a seat on the comfy chair in front of her desk, and...froze.

Looking back on it, I can imagine what was going through her head. When a military subordinate asks for a private meeting and then sits dumbstruck, visibly working up the courage to speak, it is never good news. One cannot help but play a macabre guessing game as the clock marks off the silent seconds. Divorce? Infidelity? Debt? Loss of classified documents? I can't imagine she could guess what would come next.

I managed to croak out something like "Do you know what...'transgender' means?"

She was visibly surprised but, to her credit, took it in her stride. She answered in detail; I remember her saying that she was familiar with the concept, but perhaps didn't know everything about it. She also said that she could go away and read up to understand more, and that she had an idea of where to look.

This is vitally important—a difficult skill which we value highly in my profession: the courage and composure to answer, honestly, "I don't know," not to bluster or prevaricate. That meant a great deal to me.

When she finished speaking, there was another awkward silence. I managed a rather lame joke along the lines of "Well...I'm not here because I want to discuss my annual performance review," which let us both laugh to relieve the tension.

Over and over again in future years, I would find value in good humor when discussing this stuff. If you laugh with someone, you immediately humanize them. It is very difficult to hate or fear someone who has shared a joke at their own expense with you.

The meeting ended well. I felt reassured, relieved, and supported. More importantly, I felt safe. She took pains to assure me she would protect my privacy; that she would ask consent before discussing my case with anyone. Over the next months, she did exactly that, in an almost ritualistic fashion, even if my consent could easily have been presumed from context. This was immensely valuable. We talk often about a "say–do gap" in leadership behaviors. By first undertaking to protect this very personal secret, and then visibly demonstrating her commitment to do as she had promised, achieving "say–do" parity, she engendered absolute trust in me.

As we discussed next steps and made a plan, my commander was sure that there must be official policy on gender transition in service. I was skeptical; in my head, there was almost no one else like me—certainly not in sufficient numbers to warrant an official policy! She was adamant. "We have a policy for everything. We have a policy for how often you change the locks on the filing cabinets and what clothes you're allowed to wear at the Queen's Birthday Parade. There will be a policy for this."

She was right, of course. It wasn't perfect—it has been updated twice since, and will be updated again, as our military grapples with the intricacies of pronouns, changing legal processes, and the right forms of address for non-binary superiors. But it was comprehensive, and more importantly, it was official.

I began to see a glimmer of hope for my military future. Until this point, I had been trying to reconcile two incompatible timelines: one in which I was the man I wanted to be, and a separate, distinct one in which my military career continued. I couldn't conceive successfully being a transgender army officer. The existence of this policy legitimized me. It made me a part of the machine. An unusual part, to be sure—but our military includes dog handlers, professional chefs, Olympic athletes, single parents, cancer survivors; all of them soldiers, all of them accounted for and valued. They all have their place in the great and complex bureaucracy that governs our military lives. This document made me realize for the first time the system had a place for me too.

Over the following months, I worked with my chain of command to develop a plan for my transition. Everyone has a different coming out story; there's no "right" way. I have colleagues who simply mentioned their change of gender to a few close friends and their immediate superiors and let the rumor mill do its work. I know others who took a week's administrative leave, with the unit informed officially in their absence by the commanding officer. In my case, in a small unit of about 50 soldiers who all knew me by name, we felt the best approach was to make an announcement at the weekly Friday round-up—the same time when soldiers arriving and leaving the unit were welcomed or bid farewell, and when congratulations were offered for marriages and births.

It was a nerve-wracking occasion—seasoned with a good dose of humor. My commanding officer began the announcement by formally bidding farewell to "Lieutenant W," using my old first name, and then by greeting the new commander of my detachment, "Lieutenant W." I took the time to reassure the soldiers—many of whom had never met or worked with a transgender person before—that I wasn't about to jump down their throats if they used the wrong pronoun or said "Ma'am" instead of "Sir." One of our officers had recently married, and I pointed out that we had all used her old surname for weeks after she had changed it; I expected the same errors and would treat them just as kindly.

The few seconds of silence after the announcement were some of the longest moments of my life. To my eternal gratitude, they were broken by our foreman of signals, a large, gruff man, respected and perhaps a little feared by the junior ranks, who shoved his way through the crowd to shake my hand and loudly offer me "Congratulations, sir!" It was the first time I had been called "sir" by anyone; it was a huge relief, and it immediately broke the ice. My civilian friends had been universally supportive when I came out to them, but some were a little awkward, unsure of the right protocol. "Is it okay to say congratulations?" more than one had asked. The foreman didn't bother asking, thank God. His action immediately gave permission for the rest of the room to view this as a happy occasion—putting me and, more importantly, all the junior ranks at ease.

It wasn't long before the rest of the office was happy to discuss the transition, and gently pepper me with questions—all borne out of well-meaning curiosity. Did I have to run a male time for my fitness test now? What did my husband think? Was I getting issued a male dress uniform? When would I have to start shaving? Some of the more intimate questions were the sort that, perhaps, might not pass muster as the height of courtesy in a more LGBTQ+-aware environment. I didn't mind; these people were not trying to make me feel uncomfortable—they were genuinely curious and trying to learn.

The atmosphere was helped along by my section sergeant's merciless banter; he would tell me off for trying to multitask: "You can't do that any more, sir—you made your choice," or shake his head and mutter "You've changed, sir" if he wanted to disagree with me. When I began a course of testosterone and, inevitably, had to suffer the squeak-and-boom of a voice breaking for the first time, he would get into the office early to make sure that the section telephone was placed on my desk, so that my troops could giggle at the sound of me trying not to sound like a teenager when I answered calls.

It was pure banter. It was inclusive banter, in a way I can't imagine many civilian environments could replicate. No amount of careful tiptoeing around the issue, trying not to offend, would have made me feel as included and as welcomed as the gently sarcastic ribbing of the troops who saw my transition as a target no more or less valid than another lieutenant's Wednesday afternoon cricket games, or the nearby captain's habit of sitting on an exercise ball rather than an office chair.

Taking the banter on the chin, enjoying it, and joining in, making the decision to come out publicly to my troops and, in subsequent years, making the same decision again, when I have chosen to reveal my trans identity at other units, developed me as a leader. Military organizations have not, historically, valued emotional honesty. Although this is improving, there is often a tendency to hide elements of one's personal life that might be seen as a weakness. But when I come out to my soldiers, they know immediately that I am honest and have nothing to hide. I am trusting them with intimate information, in a profession where being open about LGBTQ+ identity has, until very recently, been a significant personal risk. I show I trust them with a piece of my personal life; in turn, they know they can trust me with theirs, if they need to. They also know I won't flinch from telling them awkward or uncomfortable truths, nor hide the logic behind difficult decisions.

Once I've come out to a soldier, if I later have to give them bad news, or explain that the team will have to work long hours or take physical risk, they know it's coming from a place of personal honesty. Equally, if I compliment a soldier on their work, or tell them I'm impressed with their professionalism or their career prospects are good and they are likely to be promoted, they know I'm not just "being nice."

Coming out is an immediate and personal way to demonstrate my honesty and trust in my subordinates. That honesty and trust is very quickly reflected back at me up the power gradient. That isn't why I choose to do it; when I come out, it's because I feel more comfortable being out in the workplace, for my own wellbeing—but it is a significant added bonus.

I don't always choose to come out. For better or for worse, I began passing very well not long after I came out; it's very hard to guess I'm trans without prior knowledge. I therefore get to hear the sort of things that get said about trans people when nobody knows there's one in the room.

On one occasion, I was on pre-deployment training with two senior officers, one from my own trade. I hadn't met them before and was nervous about making a good impression. Before one of the briefs on operational safety, they began gossiping about a lecture they'd both sat through recently from a trans woman. They were speaking in the usual disparaging terms—misogynist slurs, focusing on her "mannish" appearance, all the usual bigotry.

I didn't have an opportunity to say anything before the presentation started, so I had a good half hour to collect my thoughts. (I didn't hear a word of the brief, naturally!) I sat stewing, presented with the usual adrenaline-rush catch-22 that any marginalized person will be familiar with.

Do I say something? The language they're using is unacceptable; they know it's contrary to our Army's values. I'm duty-bound to say something—and if I don't, I'll kick myself for being a coward.

But if I do speak up, am I not "making a fuss"? (A cardinal sin!)

Will they listen? If they argue back, do I out myself as trans in order to drive the point home? (And if I do, am I making the correct point—"what you're saying is wrong"—rather than the less important but more persuasive point—"what you're doing is upsetting me"?)

These men are older than me, far more senior, and I have to work in close proximity to them for at least the next week. I don't know what roles they have; one of them could be stationed two desks away from me. It's going to be horribly embarrassing and awkward if the relationship starts like this...

I eventually chose to speak up, though it was frightening. One of the officers argued back a bit; I managed to make the point clearly enough that they wouldn't (shouldn't) accept the language they'd used from their own soldiers, and I didn't need to out myself. I was ready to, but decided to hold my own status in reserve as the "silver bullet" if I couldn't make my point any other way.

Although it was a thoroughly unpleasant experience, it drove home to me how terrifying challenging a commander can be—even when you know you're in the right and have no immediate career consequences to fear. The lesson I've taken away is demonstrating (both preaching and practicing) openness to challenge in front of my own subordinates. I try to always tell new subordinates that I'm open to reasonable challenge, and I want to be told if I'm wrong; I ask them for advice and "check-zeros" regularly on small things, to ensure they are practiced in challenging me so they won't be afraid to speak up on the big things. I set the conditions carefully to ensure everyone understands the difference between reasonable challenge and insubordination, and I never mock someone for contradicting me, even if I'm right.

We all like to tell ourselves we're open to challenge, and casually use phrases like "my door is always open." But it takes an experience like this to drive home just how intimidated a junior rank can be when they want to speak up about something that has affected them personally. The easy, dismissive line is "Oh, well, if it really bothers them, they should say something." My experiences tell me that no matter how outwardly confident the soldier, if it really bothers them, they probably won't say something. On other, similar occasions, I've made the opposite call and chosen to say nothing for the sake of a quiet life. I dearly hope that no soldier has ever had to make the same choice about speaking up to me; but unless I actively work to solicit their opinions, I may never know.

Because of the luxury of passing, I'm not out by default at every workplace, as some of my trans colleagues are. I usually don't hide my identity, but it can be difficult to introduce. Coming out as gay in casual conversation is easy—I just have to say, "my husband," and can quietly declare my identity without (usually!) breaking the rhythm of small talk. Coming out as trans is much harder without suddenly turning the conversation on its head. No society has yet really normalized gender transition to the point where I can casually drop the fact I used to be a woman into a "terrible weather we're having" Monday morning workplace chat!

I have, however, deliberately hidden my identity on one occasion, when serving as a loan officer with an American unit on operations. It was in the middle of the US trans controversy, and being a gay British officer in an American headquarters already made me stand out enough: the last thing I needed was to be open about an additional queer factor which I was pretty certain wouldn't be totally welcomed!

What struck me was which of my superiors I was tempted to come out to, and why. It was shortly after I began passing easily, and I'd just deployed out of the unit where I'd transitioned, so I wasn't used to having the decision within my gift.

My immediate superior asked once about my family; he heard I had a husband, somewhat uncomfortably referred to him as my partner, and never made small talk about my background again. It was clear he was not a man I would ever feel safe coming out to. Some of the majors in the HQ (I was a junior captain) were pleasant, friendly, and open in small talk, but also very publicly expressed political opinions that I associated with anti-trans sentiment. Perhaps they would have been totally fine with it; perhaps they wouldn't. I didn't take the risk of finding out.

One officer in the HQ—a female major who had been one of the first women to complete a particularly arduous course and earn a prestigious badge, and who spoke openly and passionately about women's rights, "hit different." She mentioned gay friends in passing; phrases like "her wife" or "his husband" rolled off her tongue easily. She was very clearly comfortable with LGBTQ+ issues. She never talked about politics.

I came out to her, and only her, throughout the entire tour. It felt good to have someone know and see me for who I was. She was delighted, and very entertained that nobody had guessed.

It made me dwell on how, as leaders, we communicate a huge amount without ever intending to in everything we say and don't say, do and don't do. I don't need to say anything racist to accidentally appear unsafe to my soldiers of color—I just need to not say something at the wrong moment. I don't need to declare loudly that I'm a lazy leader to my company, I just need to walk past them when they're hard at work on a physical task, without offering to take off my jacket and jump in to help for a few minutes.

What I might think is casual workplace conversation, the clothes I wear to work, the time at night I answer emails—it all sends a message, and some of those messages are heard louder and clearer by my soldiers who are searching for someone to trust.

Since my transition, I also found a breadth of perspective, which plays to my advantage as a military leader. As an analyst and leader of analysts, I often find myself facing complex, multi-dimensional human factors problems. The experience of military service in two genders gives me two perspectives in one individual, a rare trait, though perhaps more common in those with marginalized identities who find themselves living multiple lives and embodying multiple cultural identities.

Knowing how different a room feels when it's "only boys," something I could never have experienced as a woman, and how conversations and planning cycles change when gendered perspectives are included makes me a better analyst. In turn, I dwell on the multiple perspectives my soldiers bring to the table and work harder to incorporate them. I had a tendency to homogenize before I transitioned, to assume there was a "standard Army product," and that the closer I could get my soldiers to thinking in the same way, the better. Indeed, before I transitioned I was often keen to appear as "one of the boys," not from any sense of dysphoria, but from the pressures of living as a woman in an army which (however unintentionally) acts as a locus of societal masculinity. The experience of transition totally turned that on its head. Instead, I've learned to look at where my soldiers' strengths, weaknesses, and biases lie, and build on those to create a stronger team from more diverse individuals.

I've also gained the power to intervene in sexist situations in a way I never could when I was a woman. When I observe unacceptable behavior or incidents of sexism, I can do so without seeming to make the conversation "about me," a huge taboo in my culture, where women in particular are sneered at if they seem to be putting themselves forward or acting selfishly. Now, if I hear a woman ignored, talked over, or dismissed (which I notice a lot more than my cis male colleagues!) I can intervene on her behalf and do so "cost-free." It's pure male privilege, but the trans experience allows me to weaponize it for the good of my female colleagues.

My trans identity isn't the foundation of my leadership qualities, by any means. If I'd been born male, I think (hope!) that I'd still be very much the same sort of leader. I'm an officer first, then a trans male officer, that hierarchy of identity is clear to me. But it is unquestionably another string to my bow. Just as my specific trade training, my operational experience, my social network of colleagues, and my professional education all add to my playbook, so does my trans identity. Being trans alone doesn't make me a better leader; but it does give me access to a set of perspectives and a broad emotional toolkit which I can use to improve myself and improve the lives of my soldiers.

CHAPTER 7

Shaped by the Environment

Earlier, we introduced the modern strategic leadership environment for business, warfare, and everything in between as being volatile, uncertain, complex, and ambiguous. There are rarely perfect answers and there is somehow both an overload of data and limited information. This chapter illustrates how lives lived in multiple worlds, whether closeted or out, male or female, safe or in danger, can produce valuable leadership competencies for operating in VUCA environments. Several scholars have proposed that the challenges faced by LGBTQ+ individuals may promote enhanced capacity for creativity, problem-solving, or divergent thinking - all skills that are relevant in a VUCA environment.

LGBTQ+ leaders must take stock of their environment to make decisions about how out to be. They quickly make judgments within conversations about saying wife, husband, or spouse, and consider if an activity their coworkers want to do is safe for them. In their lives they regularly must make sense of complex, variable situations using limited information. Their very existence engenders the skills to thrive in a VUCA world.

Scanning the Environment

Some people develop almost superhuman abilities to understand the world around them. Imagine hiking with a geologist who immediately grasped how every rock formation or gully you passed came to be. Think of stargazing with an astrophysicist who by looking at a star could tell you about its age, temperature, and the direction it was moving. It seems like magic. For some people, their ability to understand the world comes from reading the people around them. Just by observing, they quickly learn things others would never notice. When Bree attended graduate school, one of her classmates, Becky, had an uncanny knack for catching little signals no one else picked up on. After another student's presentation, Becky asked about a seemingly innocuous point in the presentation. The student wondered why that bit drew her attention. Becky said when he was talking about it, he got a little flush in his neck, which to her indicated something deeper was there. She was right, there was a lot more to the story, but only someone who noticed this tiny thing could have caught it. Air Force technical sergeant Andrea Herzenach said skills built through observation and coming out helped her "identify the signs of silent struggle" for her airmen, which allowed her to help provide guidance. A leader with this skill can encourage team members who may lack the confidence to share their great ideas to engage merely by recognizing them during a meeting. Some people have natural affinity for this kind of observation, others study it passionately. George Takei, who didn't come out until 68, was asked if he was afraid early in his career that others might think he was gay. He didn't think so because he was so good at hiding it, despite the amount of work it required. He said, "I was acting a part. I wasn't being paid for it, but I studied the part and I took on all the accouterments of that part."[2] Like actors, LGBTQ+ leaders can be excellent at understanding the human terrain nuances around them and adjusting accordingly.

LGBTQ+ leaders develop environment-scanning skills as a protection mechanism. If they didn't pick up on the characteristics of their environment, usually the human terrain, and act appropriately, they could be outed, beaten up, or even killed. "Before anything else, [LGBTQ+ people] have to feel safe in their environment," said Lorena Soto. "I don't think people realize how important that is and how easy it is to make queer folk feel unsafe." An anonymous contributor said, "Depending on where I'm at...I hold off on letting people know I'm part of the LGBTQ community. I get a feel for the environment to know how different people might react to the situation. It's horrible we have to worry about this." Because of that unease and need to feel safe, LGBTQ+ people hone the skills to pick up what others might miss. They watch, listen, and absorb. The downside: scanning takes effort and can be a cognitive drain. When Lindsey Medina was a military cadet, and not out, she struggled in the program because she exerted too much effort scanning. "I was so used to trying to please other people that I was putting myself second and just assessing my environment to see if I was safe or if I felt maybe I could come out," said Medina. "But that forced me to the sidelines. Other people didn't know what I was doing internally; they thought, 'She's not ready to join the conversation, or she's not ready to get the task started.'"

Amanda Fisher tells a similar story from her time at the Coast Guard Academy before coming to grips with her gender identity.

There was a running joke among a few men that I picked up on: "There goes Fisher—always aware of large predators." That jab aside, I was not ever particularly bullied. I've always been relatively popular in a niche offbeat sort of way, and would cultivate a few very close male friendships. People sort of framed me as "earnest, just always missing the mark a bit."

In social situations, especially the highly charged, hyper-competitive social environment the Academy breeds, I was more of a watcher. When I would wade in I was generally thought of as awkward, or weird, though ultimately harmless. Internally, I now recognize I was battling a sort of constant negotiation between my intense desire to simply be accepted and perform well as a man and a military officer, and the constant tug at my proverbial sleeve of That Which I Dare Not State. It was a recipe for anxiety—I assumed either everyone wrestled with these feelings, and I just wasn't handling it as well as everyone else did, or I was literally the only person in the world who felt this way.

Amanda's analogy of feeling like a prey animal is an insightful description of LGBTQ+ people scanning the environment to ensure no danger lurks in the tall grass or in the next room. However, like many traits born from negative experiences, once they were out, LGBTQ+ leaders mostly turned them into positive aspects of their lives. Austin Wilson described how his negative experiences turned into a tool he now relies upon.

Growing up gay, even if I hadn't realized it yet, forced me to become extremely adept in terms of social and emotional intelligence. Every encounter from school to church and eventually the workplace required observation and an assessment of how much of my true self I could reveal in each respective scenario. I knew if I wanted to avoid ostracism or at times even physical danger, I had to adjust my behavior according to the parameters of each unique situation. "You talk funny, are you gay?" meant I lowered my voice and talked less. "Why do you listen to girl music?" meant I hid my Hilary Duff CDs when my friends came over. While these examples seem trivial, they reflect a larger mentality that became internalized over time. Observe, assess, act accordingly. By spending so much time studying others, I learned how to identify those factors which most greatly influenced their behavior. Put another way, I learned to read the table before showing my hand. As a leader, this is an important tool because it allows me to adjust my tone, gestures, and overall demeanor according to the audience I want to reach.

Just as I used to assess the personalities of others to ensure I didn't reveal my sexuality, I can now use the same skills to elicit the intentions and motivations of my soldiers. Consequently, I am better prepared to tailor my communication to each individual and provide more relevant and genuine guidance. While my initial motivation for blending in with my surroundings was the fear of being outed, ultimately I gained the social and emotional competencies necessary to communicate effectively and relate with those around me more easily.

When scanning is turned positive, it's a critical tool for understanding audiences, reaching people where they are, and forging strong connections. Brianna Titone describes how she learned to connect with different groups:

When I worked in the environmental industry, I talked to drillers the way drillers wanted to be talked to. I told the jokes they wanted to hear. I interacted with them in different ways. When

I'm talking with executives, I talk to them in a different way. It's about trying to understand, through questioning, through listening, what is it that they want? What is interesting to them? And then focusing on those aspects.

It's playing to the audience. If I'm talking in a political event, to pro-choice people, I'm going to talk to them about what they really care about. When I'm talking to the environmentalists, I'm talking about environmental stuff. I'm not being disingenuous. I care about lots of different stuff. It's about delivering what they want to hear. I'm not going to talk to people about healthcare at an environmental rally. They don't want to hear that. They're going to tune out and they're going to say, "Forget this. I don't want to hear this." My philosophy is to find out who I'm talking to and find out what's interesting to them. Then listen, listen, listen. Before I got the courage to come out, I was ignorant about many things because I was keeping my distance and doing my own thing. I avoided the topic of the LGBT community and LGBT anything. As someone who wanted to protect myself from being outed and not really trying to understand who I was, I was afraid of even associating myself with anything LGBT, because then I might be pigeonholed in that way. Once I realized [my ignorance], I learned and listened, because one of the things good leaders do is not use their mouth all the time. It's about understanding and taking mental notes, watching other good leaders, watching the reactions people get from the words that they use, the enthusiasm in their voice, the mannerisms that they have. All of these different things can get someone to pay attention to what you're saying, get them engaged, get them to trust you.

Brianna's listen-first attitude helped her get elected and understand the needs of her constituents. She turned environmental scanning into a strength that lets her meet others where they are, build bonds, and lead effectively. The vigilance and insight developed by LGBTQ+ leaders can also allow them to utilize risk management strategies.

Risk and Opportunity Management

Risk management is about achieving goals. People all have experiences where they get knocked off track. Many times what gets us is foreseeable and risk management can help us deal with it. Basically, risk management is understanding what might occur along the way to a goal and taking action to reduce or otherwise manage the risks.

For known risks, plotting the likelihood and consequence of occurrence produces a matrix, as shown in Figure 7.1. This example shows three risks, A, B, and C, that may occur. For each risk there are five possible management strategies: Accept, Avoid, Mitigate, Transfer, or Watch. Accepting a risk means taking no action and being willing to accept the consequences if it occurs. Avoiding a risk means not taking the action that could cause the risk to be realized, or avoiding being in a situation where the risk may happen. Mitigation is taking active steps to reduce the likelihood or consequence of realizing the risk. Transference is rare—it assigns the consequence to someone or something else. Watching a risk is similar to accepting, but requires reassessment if the likelihood or consequence of the risk has changed enough to warrant switching strategies.

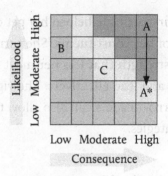

Figure 7.1 Risk Management Matrix

Closeted LGBTQ+ people often have a major goal they want to achieve: don't get outed. Risk A is being seen by someone who the LGBTQ+ person knows while they are with their partner or at an LGBTQ+ club. Being seen has a high likelihood of occurrence and an enormous consequence, so they might choose the strategy of mitigation to reduce the likelihood of occurrence to A*. How would they do this? Perhaps they'd only visit places 25 miles away from home or, for younger folks, only go out when their parents are out of town. Either strategy reduces the likelihood of being seen.

Risk B could describe a transgender person shopping for gender-affirming clothing. Though they believe the likelihood of being seen is high, the consequence is low because they have reasonable explanations, such as shopping for a gift. Because the value of getting clothing is high to them, they utilize a strategy of risk acceptance. It's also possible a combination approach has been taken to mitigate the risk, through shopping farther away from home, only shopping online, or sandwiching the clothing between other items when carried through a store.

Sabrina Bruce provides an excellent anecdote about avoidance for Risk C. Before transitioning, she was afraid to hold a purple or

a pink pen because it might give the impression she was too feminine. Sabrina wanted to be authentic and use whatever pen she
pleased but she believed one of the potential outcomes of doing so
was being identified as effeminate or transgender. By identifying
the potential consequences of her action, she stopped herself from
ever holding that pen, thus avoiding the risk ever being realized.

Austin Wilson's story provides an example of using the scanning techniques discussed previously and a risk mitigation strategy of watch. He said, "From bible study to dorm room parties,
every social situation required a sort of reconnaissance to determine how '*me*' I could be without the risk of others questioning
my masculinity, and by extension, my sexuality." He modified his
behavior until he knew enough about the circumstances to read-
just the likelihood or consequence of negative outcomes. Then, if
the risk was low enough, he could be his authentic self.

Transference is not a risk management technique often used
by closeted LGBTQ+ folks because the consequences of transference
land upon someone else. This would be done by casting doubt or
suspicion on someone else's sexuality or gender identity to take
the spotlight off the person who was initially suspected. A similar
example occurs when closeted politicians enact anti-LGBTQ+ policies as a way to transfer the risk of any suspicion that may have
been upon them to others in the community. These individuals
did not go on the journey of self-acceptance and leadership development our contributors took; instead they perpetuated negative
societal views and subsumed their own identity.

Coming out is another major source of risk management
learning. "Because coming out is taking a risk every single time, I
feel that it has been good practice for me," said Dr. Lorna Rodriguez. Research on how to explain sexuality or gender, searching
for the right setting and format to tell loved ones, and scanning

for the right time to act are some things LGBTQ+ people do when coming out. "There is that moment in a conversation when someone asks about your partner and it seems that time stops," said Bruce. "Mentally you review every interaction you have had with this person and conduct a risk analysis of sharing your status as a member of the LGBT community. As words come out of your mouth, your eyes scan their face, looking for any hint to their reaction. Would it be good or bad?"

Brooklyn Marquis said:

> I feel I have a virtual graduate degree in this stuff from all the research I did [on how to come out]! I felt like I was an expert in a lot of this stuff, because I'd done an insane amount of research on it. I tried to give myself this knowledge so I could overcome the guilt and the shame I have that's been created by society. So I over-prepared.

While Brooklyn threw energy at preparing her risk management strategy, Lorna provides a cautionary and inspiring story about continuously repeating the process:

> Showing up with your multi-hued kids, with your wife, is a form of speaking up, but it takes a lot of energy, and it is a risk. It makes you even more vulnerable, and you don't want to do that every day of your life. That's why there is an unhealthy level of stress within the lesbian community.

> It's tiring to pick and choose when to show up with your spouse, when to come out to people, yet each time I have to conceal my identity, I chisel off pieces of myself. I would love to say I stay true to myself every day but that is not the case. I intuitively pick and choose when and how to show the different layers of this onion that I am.

How do I engage in these two totally opposing behaviors (sometimes hiding and sometimes speaking up) and still deliver effective leadership? I call it survival...an acquired expertise in walking on a tightrope without falling off. And each time I do fall, I have to reconstruct myself through self-reflection, and yes, add some ice cream and chocolate to the equation!

As a leader, you need to believe in yourself and make strategic decisions about when to take risks. When in doubt, I believe you need to speak up, but at the same time, I've learned it's important to follow your instincts and make sure you stay safe.

Utilizing risk management in their personal lives informs LGBTQ+ leaders' approach in their professional capacities. Richie Jackson, author and producer, described LGBTQ+ life as inherently riskier than anything in his professional world. He said, "I'm used to risk throughout my day as a gay person, so risk in my career has never bothered me."[3] Thinking through risk mitigation in business strategies, theater productions, product launches, or military operations is similar. Disciplined processes help teams think through likelihood, consequence, and risk management strategies to enhance success.

Leaders can flip risk management around and think about opportunity management. Instead of mitigating negative outcomes, opportunity management thinks about enhancing positive outcomes by raising the likelihood or consequence of opportunities. Imagine a business with a key parts supplier. In risk management, they'd think about ensuring parts are delivered on time, ensuring cost stability, or what to do if their supplier goes out of business. Conversely, an opportunity manager might think about scanning the market for better deals, investing to create additional suppliers, or redesigning the component to no longer require suppliers.

Kris Moore's opportunity was to speak in front of the Secretary of Defense and many senior Pentagon leaders at a Department of Defense Pride event. He could have easily said no, but saw the opportunity for what it was: a chance to highlight contributions of transgender service members to people who make decisions about their futures in the military. He looked for ways to improve his chances of success. He reached out to mentors and got advice on the speech, he practiced again and again, and he gave himself the confidence to stand proudly on stage. "Did I think more than once about calling in sick? Absolutely, but I always get stage fright," said Moore. "I'm very grateful that I had that opportunity to get up there and share my story and to see so many admirals and generals."[4] His opportunity management process allowed him to shine.

Opportunity management is still a risk-taking process; almost nothing is a sure bet. LGBTQ+ leaders may fail when making bets, but they've got the courage to make them and the resilience to rebound. When opportunities pay off they can result in huge wins for individuals and organizations. Sabrina Bruce recalled the opportunity coming with her transition and the courage required to own it. She said, "Transition is about claiming your identity. You are faced with a decision in life and you must have faith it's the right decision. It is an opportunity but you must have the courage to go all in and claim it."

Coming out experiences are easily reframed as turning risk management into opportunity management. Jess Warren put it simply: "If I hadn't been given the opportunity to come out I would not have been able to spread my wings and make the impact I have." Electrical engineering manager Liam Connors Smith hid who he was as a queer trans man for the first 15 years of his career. For all that time he feared his work quality would be judged negatively if he came out, but he was disconnected from his peers. His coming out was the opportunity to fix that. "Coming out gave me the opportunity to really get to know people, and for people to feel like they could get to know me, and in some cases that they could trust me more now," he said. He's happier, better connected, and more productive now.

Perspective-Taking

Developmental crucibles push individuals to challenge their views and make sense of the world in new ways: a disruptive experience at the heart of vertical development. Leaders at higher levels of mental complexity can take and hold multiple diverse, even seemingly competing perspectives. Their ability to take themselves off the stage and up to the balcony to observe the play of events around them lets them synthesize information and make sense of what's happening.[5]

Anderson and Ackerman Anderson (2013) say that leaders at higher levels of complexity "see interdependencies that others miss, feel more confident in the face of unknown dilemmas, and can more effectively solve challenges that seem to possess irreconcilable differences and polarities."[6] They identified how this capacity enables effectiveness in VUCA environments: "The wider a leader's perspective across systems, the more they can see the order in chaos, handle greater complexity, make sense of emergent novelty, listen to diverse points of view, and perceive the interconnectedness of myriad dynamics."[7] We believe this to be what makes LGBTQ+ leaders so effective in today's world.

What LGBTQ+ people go through to develop multiple perspectives has positive and negative aspects. One of those experiences is code-switching. Code-switching is a version of identity management where people present different versions of themselves in different contexts. Many minorities code-switch when in some contexts they speak or act the way they believe others expect them to, such as in the workplace, but in other contexts act authentically.

Michelle Macander described several negative situations in her life as code-switching. Her mother told her not to come out to her grandparents and "let them die thinking you're straight" so she acted differently around them. She also said there are parts of the world and America where she wouldn't hold her wife's hand in public. Those experiences cause her to be a bit more self-reflective and observant than she might otherwise be. Still, recognizing situations and modifying behavior to get desired outcomes is translatable to leadership contexts.

Transgender people hold multiple perspectives in ways not easily accessible to cisgender people. Their perspectives of different genders can provide additional impetus to vertical development. Many minorities develop abilities to see multiple perspectives but transgender individuals, more so transgender people of color, have many layers of identity, allowing them to relate to others' perspectives and vision. Raffi Freedman-Gurspan, the first trans White House staffer, has championed human rights in the government and nonprofit sectors for over a decade. She utilizes her many intersectional identities in her advocacy work. "In my faith tradition, leaders like Moses and Queen Esther are ambassadors, or go-between liaisons with various communities," said Freedman-Gurspan. "They can step back and see the bigger picture. That's what sustains me. I can see many vantage points, and I can help both sides to see the broader picture; that is something needed right now in our society."

Blake Dremann described his transition in this way:

I no longer held a single perspective. I wasn't just a white male. I had experienced the military as a female who integrated an all-male space [submarines] and a gay female who came out after the repeal of DADT. I possess many perspectives that allow me to challenge old perceptions by now being in the space of power. It is a unique position.

In figuring out how to act, underrepresented people often walk into a meeting and count the room to see how many others like them are present, some doing so almost subconsciously because environmental scanning is so ingrained. They are accustomed to being one of the few, or the only one, like themselves in the room. Someone like Blake may never count the room again. However, for a white transgender woman, it's a new experience and something she likely never did when the world perceived her as a man. Because of these nuances, environment scanning becomes a conscious process. By examining the process and the consciousness shift, transgender people can build empathy and see challenges from more than one angle.

"I work in military analysis, and the presence of multiple perspectives on a problem is always a superpower in the sort of complex human-factors problems I find myself facing," said Harry Walter. "Having the experience of serving as both a woman and a man in the Army has given me two perspectives in one individual—a rare trait, and one which only marginalized identities can really boast."

Transgender people's privilege changes based on their transition, adding another perspective. For transgender women, it can be a similar experience to coming out for an LGBQ+ person in losing an aspect of privilege they previously carried, consciously or not. For transgender men, it's opposite—privilege is thrust upon them. "I was no longer the minority member," said Dremann. "I am a straight white male with passing privilege. This gave me opportunities. More male colleagues seemed to be open to mentoring me. I was given more leeway in meetings to challenge the status quo." This massive change in interpersonal dynamics is another opportunity for growth and empathy development.

Kris Moore offers a poignant example of how his perspectives have shifted and how leaders can help develop the ability of others to broaden their perspectives:

Transitioning taught me how much we need to be allies for women and minorities. When I was a [female] midshipman I said, "We need to stop bringing attention to ourselves and just do our jobs. We don't need to keep making a big deal about being women." Once I transitioned and passed as a man, I noticed how easy it was. No longer was I called a bitch when I told people what to do, gave orders, handed out tasks. I wasn't constantly asked if it was that time of the month. I wasn't told I was being emotional. People finally just did what I said, and if I raised my voice, people knew it was for a reason. People didn't speak over me, call me honey, or tell me to simmer down. People respected me for who I was. I quickly realized that I was respected as a man and not as a person, because I never felt this respect as a woman.

The first thing that comes to mind [about teaching perspectives] is sea stories. A sea story is like "This last time when I was on deployment, we did this, that and the other." When a junior sailor is looking to their chief petty officer for advice on something, the chief doesn't just answer the question. What they're going to do is go into a story. They'll talk about their

SHAPED BY THE ENVIRONMENT

own experience or the experience of their friends and that sailor is going to get drawn in and listen to every word.

When we tell stories, we create imagery and an experience others can insert themselves into and visualize what it would be like for them. I share my experiences because, as a teacher, students don't want to be lectured at. When you plug through PowerPoint it's like, "Oh, this is horrible." When you share experiences and allow others to ask questions about that experience, it gets the conversation going so it's not a one-way lecture.

Diversity [of perspective] promotes success because you've got different folks looking at things from different angles and providing inputs. Person A can see it from the upper left and person C can see it from the bottom right. They can talk to each other about "Hey, this is what I'm seeing over here. Are you seeing this?" Diversity allows the team to come together and take the right path because you're getting more than one way to look at the situation.

If you can be disciplined in making yourself look at situations from different angles, especially if you've had experience in those positions, you can not only help others, but you can drive success for yourself because you're more likely to find the most efficient path toward mission accomplishment.

Multiple perspectives are critical to mission accomplishment. Looking at things from different angles in team environments necessitates bringing others in to share perspectives and develop better solutions.

Each leadership capacity discussed in this chapter illuminates how LGBTQ+ leaders come to see the world differently.

Fundamentally, seeing and understanding more is the essence of vertical development. Once leaders develop these skills, often because of the need for safety, they direct their enhanced sight toward the challenges in front of them. Like magic, these superpowers enable them to comprehend and examine much more of the complex environments where they live and lead.

CHAPTER 8

Always Growing

Lifelong learning, continuous growth, and transformation are frequently emphasized as essential leadership qualities in today's tumultuous environment. LGBTQ+ experiences foster abilities to learn, grow, and improve continually: activities essential to effective leadership in complex contexts. Seeing the limits of current thinking for facing a person's demands prompts cognitive growth. Impetus for change arises from disequilibrium, or a feeling of being out of balance, when we realize the limits of our current ways of thinking.[1] For example, most people start adulthood guided by expectations from the important people or groups in their life. They gain certainty and comfort from meeting these standards and receiving external validation. However, eventually expectations may conflict or become untenable—causing uncertainty and instability. Some adults recognize that staying beholden to others' expectations is not an ideal path. This recognition may let them develop alternative ways of thinking, such as developing their own standards and gaining comfort from internal validation. Experiencing demanding and complex environments, or facing crucible moments, often kickstarts this process.

Let's explore the qualities that enable continuous learning and self-improvement in LGBTQ+ journeys: growth mindsets, motivation, and resilience.

Growth Mindsets

Psychologist Carol Dweck researched how attitude and motivation relate to why people succeed or fail, and whether they keep trying, which showed a difference in *mindset*.[2] According to Dweck, a mindset is a set of beliefs about whether individual characteristics such as intelligence, personality, and creativity are permanent or able to be developed. People with fixed mindsets believe they are born with a set of characteristics that cannot be altered, so they are stuck with what they've got. As such, they are more likely to avoid challenges, give up easily, disregard feedback, and hide or minimize deficiencies. Conversely, people with growth mindsets believe their inborn characteristics are a starting point that can be enhanced through effort. They readily accept challenges, setbacks, and feedback; apply energy to learn, grow, and adapt; are more open to change; and will identify and take advantage of development opportunities. Later stages of adult cognitive development are more mentally complex; are subject to less biases and assumptions; have broadened vantage points; and are better able to take perspectives, embrace paradox and ambiguity; and view the self as continually evolving or transforming—indicative of growth mindsets. Leaders with these qualities are more open, willing to question prior assumptions and knowledge, and likely to be lifelong learners. Growth mindsets may be fostered by LGBTQ+ experiences such as code-switching, revising membership groups, or repeatedly coming out. For example, many LGBTQ+ individuals faced unaccepting or hostile family or hometown dynamics, forcing them to leave their place of origin to seek safer or more accepting communities. This requires navigating changing circumstances by adapting how they express themselves, relate to others, operate in different environments, and exhibit their identity.

Louis Swanson beautifully described the growth mindset within transgender experiences:

> In kindergarten, I had a simple, somewhat vague idea of who I would be as an adult. I knew society expected me to be something different than anything that matched my ideal self. I was expected to do great things. But the great things were to be done by a woman. I was horrible at being a girl, and had no interest in trying. I found it nearly impossible to envision my adult self as happy and successful—as a woman. Still, even in kindergarten, I had the audacity to believe, somehow, I would find a way to be the best version of myself. I am proud to say I have accomplished that goal.

A fixed mindset could have limited Louis' possibilities, whereas a growth mindset enabled hope, belief in self, and eventually transformation.

Sabrina Bruce also articulated how pre-transition experiences inculcated an openness to learn and grow:

> Before I transitioned, I didn't want anybody to get the impression I was too feminine. Now I can just be who I am. I don't have to worry about any of that. I understand whenever there's a mistake or I've done something wrong, and it's okay to admit it because growth comes from those mistakes. It comes from admitting to myself and to others that this is not right and I'm going to be better.

Jennifer Finney Boylan described this growth as a belief in revision. She said:

> The biggest thing I have (certainly as a writer, but also in other ways) is belief in *revision*. If you don't get something right the

first time, your life isn't over. To be willing to admit that any belief you have might be wrong, to be willing to have your mind changed, to be open to new knowledge. What is being transgender if not a kind of cosmic way of believing in the power of multiple drafts? Being trans made me understand you get a lot of shots in this life. It's never too late to become yourself.[3]

Beyond how someone interprets what they were born with, considering transition requires deep introspection and self-awareness. Ideally, this develops commitments to be true to oneself and reach for continued improvement. Reaching the internal conclusion that an individual isn't yet their best self requires a growth mindset. It's a commitment to change on a fundamental level and difficult to achieve without a growth mindset and fully developed self-authoring mind. Transition inherently includes belief in a better future self and the potential to reach beyond one's current capacity.

Motivation

LGBTQ+ leaders, like other marginalized individuals, have worked incredibly hard to prove themselves, gain access to opportunities, receive acknowledgement or recognition, and earn the respect of colleagues. Without exceptional motivation and drive, achieving leadership roles would likely be impossible. LGBTQ+ leaders need to overcome marginalization, redirect others' attention, earn their place, or even prove others' misconceptions wrong, motivating them to not give up. "Hiding my identity probably did help me with my career progression because I always worked harder than my peers in an attempt to prove and solidify my worth to service out of fear that if I did any less I would have leadership coming after me," said Space Force colonel Meredith Beg.

Michelle Macander made a point of proving herself to male counterparts. After taking command of the 1st Combat Engineering Battalion, she led her Marines on a forced march. Afterwards, several Marines told her they couldn't believe someone so small could seemingly easily set a challenging pace. Michelle's example is one way minorities drive themselves to exceed both standards and perceptions. "There was a lot of internal pressure to make sure I fit the culture by working as hard as I could," said Macander, continuing:

> It made me a better leader because I felt I had something to prove, which may not be very healthy and it's probably not fair. But that's something that I did for myself and it made me a much more capable leader because I didn't want myself to fail, not just for me, but because of those that are coming behind me and what my leadership represents.

Dominic Longo articulated the desire to grow:

> There is like a gravitational pull developmentally in being queer. There's something that pulls us forward to grow, to change, to claim ourselves. Which is a gift and a burden. And yet, of course there's a developmental pull forward for every human being. It just has a different flavor and contour for queer folks and we have built in obstacles in the design of society and its conventions. We're all called to be ourselves and to become ourselves ever more fully, which is a never-ending process. As long as we're alive.

Resilience

Remaining motivated in the face of adversity requires a wellspring of energy renewal and the ability to rebound after inevitable setbacks and losses. LGBTQ+ leaders show resilience through surviving and recovering from adversity and learning from those experiences to thrive. Resilience, defined as "the process of adapting well in the face of adversity, trauma, tragedy, threats or significant sources of stress," may be the most ubiquitous characteristic of LGBTQ+ leaders.[4] Being a leader almost guarantees they've overcome and rebounded from adversity. Austin Wilson said:

> Being an LGBTQ+ leader means being resilient. Not the kind of resilience that can be taught, but rather the kind that stems from generations of being beaten down, demonized, and altogether disregarded. LGBTQ+ leaders know how to form networks and blend in to any type of crowd because our very survival used to depend on it.

Austin describes resilience at the level of essential survival instinct—essentially a quality that *must* be developed.

Ross Murray knows the importance of turning rejection into resilience:

> Recognize that rejection is one moment. Rejection from one party doesn't mean the world has rejected me. It doesn't mean I have lost all my family, friends, and support network. It doesn't stop it from hurting, and it doesn't stop it from stinging, but it's part of this much larger constellation that can help put [the rejection] into perspective.

Retired Air Force major general Trish Rose, the first out lesbian to attain that rank, says resilience is not an option, but an imperative.

Early in her career her commander was giving out additional duties. The men got substantive jobs; she was asked to be the party planner. It was her springboard to resilience; she spoke up, and said it was the beginning of her philosophy: "You can be pitiful, or you can be powerful, but you can't be both." She frames resilience as a requirement to stand up for oneself when others will surely attempt to knock you down.

Angela Duckworth describes resilience as our ability to bounce back after having struggled, being able to pick ourselves up, dust ourselves off, collect ourselves, and continue moving forward.[5] It's unlikely LGBTQ+ leaders could have ascended to their positions without facing obstacles directly related to their LGBTQ+ status and building the resilience necessary to recover from setbacks. Sabrina Bruce's transition enabled development of a powerful internal narrative:

> When my hair was short and I hadn't quite grown into my features, I had to walk around in public when all I wanted to do was stay in my room and let my hair grow and let myself change into the person I knew I was. I felt ashamed. Ashamed I didn't meet the standards I held for myself and the expectations I had. But I still had to do it. As I walked, I would realize, hey, I'm in my own head. Nobody here is thinking about me. Nobody's caring about me. They're all dealing with their own things... Each time I stepped out of my door, I got a little stronger and realized I could deal with these situations.

The American Psychological Association recommends that people build resilience by accepting that change is constant, knowing bad things will happen, learning about ourselves, and getting control over how we respond to adverse events.[6] Many LGBTQ+ individuals learned these lessons early, often, and as a matter of survival. Ross Murray said:

> I spend time thinking up the worst possible thing that can happen because once you imagine that, you find a lot of stuff that falls short of the worst possible thing. Or at least it's not a surprise. I don't want people to feel caught off guard by rejection that they didn't expect.

Lorena Soto's adversity came with great loss, significant personal and professional consequences, and a lot of pain and baggage. "To work through self-hate and self-doubt, it's learning how to think again," explained Soto:

> There's work I put into it, in the morning I have to wake up and decide. I have worksheets where I have to write down what kind of day I'm going to have and who I'm going to be today. It challenges me every single day. It's important as a leader in the queer community to acknowledge that. To acknowledge that this experience that I'm having is not unique at all, especially for my trans siblings. Overcoming the self-hate, overcoming addiction... The only way we knew how to cope was to drink and do drugs. A lot of us come with baggage. In order to develop our queer leadership you have to deal with the baggage... It requires work on yourself and that is serious work every day. I'm re-teaching myself how to think, how to process love, self-acceptance, all of that, because you're not taught that.

Similarly, Cory Newell shared how challenging it is to work through the pain of others' and one's own baggage about identity:

> I've had to learn to adapt, that my identity doesn't rest in that person's ideal of what my identity should be, my identity

is what I identify as... And just because you can't put your mind around that, that doesn't bother me. But it took about three years to get to that place. I still struggle with parts of it.

These examples illustrate a chosen path to continue moving forward while overcoming massive obstacles. Whether it's finding the motivation to continue despite the exhaustion of dealing with constant marginalization, or summoning the resilience to get back up after being knocked down—these leaders somehow find the energy and strength to keep going. Further, they transform these experiences into enhanced capacities that make them better leaders and allow them to support others.

LGBTQ+ leaders develop and embody essential leadership qualities that enable continuous learning and self-improvement: growth mindsets, motivation, and resilience. These ideas are a prelude to how LGBTQ+ leaders help inspire others. Ross Murray explained:

Queer leadership is people that have been through things and know how to be leaders for others. If you look at the experiences of people who come from the margins, our society doesn't often call that leadership. But people have been able to survive and thrive even with limited resources; you can see incredible leadership coming out of marginalized communities. The queer community is part of that. [Especially within] the intersections, you're going to find that leadership comes up because people are very acutely aware of how the world works. They have figured out solutions for themselves and can be really good at helping other people figure out solutions.

CHAPTER 9

All about Others

LGBTQ+ leaders extensively cite authenticity, vulnerability, and honesty as key tools inherently and necessarily developed on their journeys. As today's leaders recognize, these leadership capacities develop trust, build psychological safety, and enhance collaboration. According to Paul Dinte, chairman of IIC Partners, "Today's most valued senior executive is not...a talented practitioner. Rather, this sought-after executive is very 'other-directed' and excels at harnessing the power of others through leadership and inspiration."[1] LGBTQ+ leaders draw on their own experiences to focus outward and develop others instead of taking a self-centered view of leadership.

Journeys to authenticity catalyze the development of empathy, caring, perspective-taking, listening, and understanding. These skills are essential but uncommon in many professional contexts because they are not naturally fostered and promoted by many workplaces and industries, especially those that emphasize individual contribution, advancement, and competition. Traditional professional settings tend to foster heroic leadership behaviors such as autocratic, unilateral decision-making, whereas today's complex challenges require a post-heroic participatory leadership approach, characterized by humility, facilitation, question-asking, and inclusivity.[2] As such, learning how LGBTQ+ leaders develop and hone these capacities provides valuable insights for all leaders.

LGBTQ+ journeys' hard-fought and hard-won self-acceptance organically extends to other-acceptance. Self-development of authenticity, vulnerability, and honesty enhances development of other-focused capacities such as empathy, listening and understanding, collaboration and inclusion, mentoring and empowering, modeling behavior, and inspiring others: a powerful theme to be accessed by all leaders.

From Self to Other

Does the development of authenticity, vulnerability, and honesty in turn enhance a leader's ability to develop other-focused capacities? LGBTQ+ experiences indicate an interplay between developing the self and helping others. Contributors described this interplay in terms of energy and space gained to support others after progressing in their journeys. By living authentic lives, having shed the weight of being closeted or struggling with fear, these leaders gained back much of themselves to pour into others. "Going from a space in the closet, to coming out took down my guard," said Cory Newell. "If I can't love myself in a space of who I am in my own trueness...then I'm never, ever, ever going to be able to have a genuine space with other people."

Kris Moore and Kristian Johnsen echoed a similar sentiment: coming out was essential to freeing up energy that can be channeled into helping others. "Coming out as a lesbian and then transgender allowed me to live my authentic self, not hide or cover up who I was on the weekends, or be socially awkward when we talked about personal life," said Kris. Kristian explained:

Taking that unnecessary weight off my shoulders allowed me the energy and time to focus on my sailors and my job. Coming out allowed me to be my full, authentic self and develop deeper relationships with my coworkers. It pushed me to be vulnerable and forced me to overcome my fears of what impact my identity might have on my career. It allowed me to devote energy previously devoted to monitoring my every word to my airmen instead.

Blake Dremman illustrates the benefits of authenticity through coming out and how transition enables enhanced capacities for empathy and humility:

Coming out helped me be more authentic and allowed me to develop leadership skills, because I wasn't trying to necessarily go unnoticed. There were a few things I noticed immediately. I was no longer the minority member. I am a straight white male with passing privilege. This gave me opportunities and male members of the military seemed to be open to mentoring me from the perspective of being a white male. I was given more leeway to challenge the status quo. It came about by being perceived as a white male.

But superpowers developed. Empathy was one of them. I no longer held a single perspective. The other is humility. I wasn't focused on telling my story, but elevating others' stories, because I had such an over-privileged experience. I also became aware that my words had power and I had to be super aware of how my words were perceived and received. It was also on me to motivate those who needed extra encouragement.

These examples illustrate how authenticity creates opportunities to devote more energy to helping others. While these stories relate specifically to coming out, anyone can relate to the experience. Whenever people practice identity management, trying to display an external image different from internal truth, they experience the same tradeoff.

Overcoming Adversity and Paying It Forward

LGBTQ+ experiences often develop capabilities to identify and respond to the needs of others. Sometimes this capability develops by being cared for and supported in their most challenging times, fortifying their desire to pay it forward. In others, lack of support for their own challenges motivates them to do better for others. Tamara Adrian said:

Nobody actually wants or decides to be an LGBTI person. It's the destiny you have to face. You are so fearful of what might become of you. We are forced to help those who are coming behind us to accept who they are and make it somehow easier for them to be accepted, to come out of the closet. That has been a driving force for me.

From negative and positive experiences, these leaders develop and employ essential other-focused leadership qualities.

For some leaders, hardship experienced through lack of support or overt marginalization provides clarity on what others may need and how to provide it. Kris Moore said:

I've been looked at and talked to differently. I empathize with people... I know what it feels like to be treated differently because I don't fit society's little box of what is expected. That allowed me to...give people a chance, a seat at the table...you've got to empathize and understand they've been trying but we're not giving them that opportunity because they're not the first person that comes to mind.

Savannah Hauk described how the risk of facing adversity enables the ability to support others: "By exposing my gender identity I can be an effective leader for others who may still feel alone, in the closet, shrouded in shame, and unable to find others who celebrate their identities."

Some leaders grow through compassion and support provided by others. The care they received fortified them and enabled them to do the same for others. Jennifer L. Dane is compassionate with others and listens intentionally, even when it's exhausting:

> We don't know people's stories, we don't know their journeys or how they feel. Just be there to listen, and listen with your whole heart. Sometimes you can help them, sometimes you can't. Because people showed me so much compassion, I do that for others. I feel like it's an obligation. That's at the root of how I lead.

Apple CEO Tim Cook wrote:

> Being gay has given me a deeper understanding of what it means to be in the minority and provided a window into the challenges that people in other minority groups deal with every day. It's made me more empathetic, which has led to a richer life.

He went on to discuss his inspiration for paying it forward:

> When I arrive in my office each morning, I'm greeted by framed photos of Dr. King and Robert F. Kennedy. I don't pretend that writing this puts me in their league. All it does is allow me to look at those pictures and know that I'm doing my part, however small, to help others. We pave the sunlit path toward justice together, brick by brick. This is my brick.[3]

Paying it forward resonates throughout LGBTQ+ communities.

Almost everyone we spoke with considered it part of their reason for contributing to this work. Their tremendous sense of responsibility provides a constant impetus to keep helping. Sharing their stories is one more way to develop and support others.

Empathy

Developing empathy was one of the most common themes of our interviews, which is why it's inseparably woven into other sections. LGBTQ+ leaders' struggles translated into empathy for the difficulties others face, even when they didn't know what those difficulties were. Virginia House of Delegates member Danica Roem, the first openly transgender person elected to a state legislature, said:

> I didn't get this far so I could start discriminating against other people. I know what it's like to have to overcome hurdles that were designed for me to fail… When you have that perspective that gives you much more insight into wanting to be not only inclusive, but wanting to take the initiative to get to know other people. You're looking for the hurt they don't necessarily express or show. You understand people may be masking something that they are too afraid to express, and have their own reason, their own journey. The skill sets you develop recognize the things that caused that hurt and how to apply the balm to soothe that hurt.

Russ Houser developed an inward empathy he projects outward as well. "What was really helpful was learning to be gentle with myself. That translated to being gentle with other people too, giving them room to make mistakes, giving them space so that they knew it was all right." Cory Newell articulated this empathetic capacity as acceptance:

Being in a queer space allows me to accept all things and all people as they are, whether they want purple aliens as their divine, or Jesus Christ Superstar, it doesn't matter... And that ability to love and to see past or to look through, allows a place of compassion.

Dayna Walker believes a leader's role, through empathy, is creating positive impacts, even when things have gone wrong:

The biggest thing is empathy and understanding... We expect our leaders to look at everything holistically, understand what's going on, and help people with whatever situation they have, even if they stepped over the line or got in trouble. Our job is to help them solve the situation, put them back on the track if we can, rehab them, whatever we need to do... What we're looking for as leaders are positive outcomes. We have more positive outcomes by being treated as who we are, and being able to use our full range of experiences in a way that is going to augment others as they expect us to augment them.

This empathetic capacity helps leaders create open and accepting spaces for others to share their challenges. Brianna Titone said:

So many people want to share their story with me and tell me what's happening to them...because they need help... I take a lot of the weight that they bear on myself. A lot of other LGBT leaders also do that. It's really sad what happens to a lot of people, and we don't want to see that continue to happen. It's empathy that helps us deliver leadership.

Empathetic leaders become sounding boards and safe spaces for those who are struggling—in any way. In holding this space, they also must be equipped to listen deeply and truly understand those they aim to support.

Listening and Understanding

LGBTQ+ leaders know how important it is to understand what others are going through. Because they frequently faced difficulty resulting from others' lack of understanding or awareness of their own struggles, they developed enhanced capacity to listen for the needs of those they lead.

"To really understand the different ways people are affected by the identities they hold, you have to look into it, listen to all those different things, and understand where people are coming from," said Brianna Titone. "It's always been about trying to understand, through questioning, through listening, what is it that they want? What's interesting to them? And then focus on those aspects… Listen, listen, listen."

Many leaders ask questions to dig a bit deeper into understanding what others might be going through. Sabrina Bruce explained:

> When I approach somebody, when they've come late to work, when they're a little bit down at their desk and not joking or happy, like they usually are—I understand I don't need to yell at them that they're late or berate them for being lazy. I need to ask them, *"Hey, what's going on?"* Because I remember those same moments where I had a breakdown, and I was just silently melting down, and things were falling apart around me but on the outside, it seemed like nothing was wrong at all. I was holding it all inside.

Sabrina's approach is an excellent way to let people know they are cared about as individuals, not as the tasks they perform. It opens the door to enhanced connection and helps dig beyond surface issues to address root causes.

Similarly, Dayna Walker's unique vantage points enable her to ask questions others don't:

> From a gender standpoint, [my intersex experience] allows me to bridge gaps that normally wouldn't be there, to bring forth understanding of how people may perceive different situations based on their gender or based on their experiences. Leaders need to dig down and ask, "Hey, are you doing this because of this or that?"...questions I'm more ready to ask because of my experiences.

Collaboration and Inclusion

Leaders' capacity for listening and understanding allows them to help those who are struggling and enables them to perform the essential work of creating opportunities for inclusion and collaboration. Lindsey Medina's enhanced empathy developed her ability to make space and bring others in and draw the best out of people:

> My journey made me extremely empathetic, inclusive, and welcoming of people who struggle to connect in easily identifiable ways. When I meet someone, I try to determine how we are going to connect. You can't stop at the surface level of "we don't have anything in common."
>
> Listening to people's needs and listening to what people can do saves a lot of energy... Every person is so different from each other that if you hold them all to the same standard, they're going to inevitably fail. I'm not asking for anyone's best by my standards, I'm asking for their best by their standards. That

takes energy to figure out... Every person has a different ceiling, and that's okay...but that energy and work is always worth it. Down the road after you've built a connection with them and built trust, they're going to give you their best work because they know you're worth it.

If you get to know people, listen to them, and include them... when they're comfortable, and feel safe, they're going to open up and start connecting with you.

Jennifer L. Dane, talking about bringing people in, said, "I try to make room at the table and pull up a seat. Or, if the table isn't working, completely destroy the table and figure out a new table. Or, not even a table at all." This illustrates how LGBTQ+ leaders develop sophisticated leadership capacities to respond to the unique needs and challenges of their group.

Mentoring and Empowering

LGBTQ+ leaders' inclusive approach is often built upon their experiences of having their voice elevated by others or by their recognition of how important it is to develop those who come behind them. Therefore, mentoring is a huge part of LGBTQ+ leadership approaches.

Contributors spoke in detail about their desire to lift others up and leave a lasting and positive impact on those they lead and mentor. This theme resonated through stories about leading subordinates, mentoring teammates, empowering youth, and pushing for social change. Having been through incredibly challenging self-development journeys, they are eager and passionate about empowering those following them.

"I like to one-on-one mentor," shared Kris Moore. "It's beautiful to be able to help...to be able to tell people, 'Hey, it's going to be okay'...to calm them down, get them to take deep breaths and get them grounded. I love stuff like that." Kris applies empathy and caring to the deliberate leadership practice of mentoring.

Beyond mentorship, LGBTQ+ leaders enable others to succeed and create positive change by opening doors and creating space. "I want to use the position I have in the best way I can, make the most of my tenure here, help the most people, inspire people, and lift people up with me," said Brianna Titone. Similarly, Kristian Johnsen said, "It's rewarding any time you can make the path a little bit easier for those that come behind you...to help take care of and to mentor, and to help them get what they need to be successful."

Jennifer L. Dane described a perpetual cycle of mentoring and empowering, enabling people to enable others. When working with young people, she said:

> I want them to see there's at least one adult that cares so much about them, and wants them to be there. Because there's going to be somebody else that they need to be there for. If I can do that, if I can be that one caring adult in their life, at the end of the day that's important. I care enough to know they need to be here to help carry on for others.

Contributors highlighted the importance of providing mentoring that enables other members of marginalized communities to succeed. Lorena Rodriguez shared that:

> My goal is to mentor new leaders, young people, young people of color, young queer people to take over. Our youth are amazing right now. The way these kids are taking to the streets and standing up, it's beautiful. Most of the protests and events I've gone to have been organized and led by young people.

Whenever they reach out to me, I'm like, what do you need me to do? I will do whatever is needed to make this easier for you.

Like Lorena, Lindsey Medina believes it's her responsibility to empower future leaders:

I'm trying to open the door and keep it open...let me show you how I was able to accomplish it so that maybe you can either repeat that, or you can build on it. We're not just here to fade in the background, not get what we want, and not develop. We're equal, we deserve the same amount of attention and leadership development.

There's a strong sense of responsibility, perhaps even obligation, felt by LGBTQ+ leaders to help others in their community.

Modeling Behavior

In addition to ensuring doors are open, and giving people the support and encouragement needed to walk through them, LGBTQ+ leaders are examples their mentees can follow. Authenticity and self-expression are important ways leaders enable others through modeling. Dr. Kati McNamara, a bisexual Air Force social worker said, "When in doubt, come out. There are people anxiously observing whether any higher-ranking people are out. Once you come out, so many will follow your lead, and you'll feel like a badass leader who's improving people's ability to be their authentic selves."

Retired major general Tammy Smith modeled behavior to help others take their own steps forward:

I helped the Army understand being out wasn't a political statement, it was simply a statement of authenticity. I wasn't being an activist by being out, I was simply being honest about my family composition. As I made my way through things, such as my wife Tracey's participation in my promotion ceremony, I created a model for others to follow and use within their own commands. For example, when a person in a married same-sex relationship wanted their spouse to participate in a promotion ceremony or be part of a change of command ceremony they could leverage my own ceremony and say, "This is what General Smith did, we are going to use the same script."

Julie Janson described helping others develop understanding:

I channel all the things I wish someone had said or done for me when I felt voiceless and I unapologetically make it known where I stand on discrimination, sexual assault, and harassment. Because what happened to me was so awful and dark it supercharges me to prevent it from happening to anyone else. I learned from my experience that it's hard to know who is on your side, so I am very public about my support. I make my pronouns known, I wear my Pride clothes to events, I sing RuPaul songs...anything I can do to broadcast to the people around me "*I got you, you're not alone.*" I believe this had the unintended effect of increasing the authenticity with which I approach the world, which feels like a superpower in and of itself. Wonderfully, through public displays I've had more and more members of the predominant culture come to me with tough questions. I hope that in small ways, me having these conversations gives breathing room to those who aren't ready to have them.

Inspiring Others

Modeling authenticity provides people an example to follow,

enables their journey to authenticity, and touches hearts. In Tim Cook's coming out letter, he wrote:

> I believe deeply in the words of Dr. Martin Luther King, who said: "Life's most persistent and urgent question is, 'What are you doing for others?'" I often challenge myself with that question, and I've come to realize that my desire for personal privacy has been holding me back from doing something more important... So if hearing that the CEO of Apple is gay can help someone struggling to come to terms with who he or she is, or bring comfort to anyone who feels alone, or inspire people to insist on their equality, then it's worth the trade-off with my own privacy.[4]

Melissa Gumbs also expressed this sentiment:

> I get a lot of direct messages from Sint Maarteners who have left the island saying, "I'm so happy and proud to see an openly lesbian woman in our Parliament. I didn't think that I'd ever see this day and it gives me hope and it makes me want to consider coming back home." So I look at my presence as providing them with a vision of what it could be like.

LGBTQ+ leaders inspire other LGBTQ+ people, the individuals they lead and mentor, and anyone who observes them. "Being fully authentic as a non-binary person in my role has led to opportunities for people who report to me, or see me as a potential mentor, to find a safe space in me as a leader for authentic expression of, and exploration of their own identities," said Jess Warren. "I've become more confident in using my own voice—changing from a timid introvert who avoids attention, to embracing the discomfort to bring my valuable voice to the table, and enabling the valuable voice of others who I can support through their journeys."

Jess' leadership projects inspiration and encouragement and magnetically pulls people in, prompting new opportunities for mentorship and empowerment.

Sabrina Bruce aptly described how displaying authenticity and vulnerability enables others to open up and share their own struggles:

> When you're true to yourself, you're able to be true to those around you and share every bit of yourself without having any reservations... I believe looking weak is okay. I think that shows who you are. I know I've broken down before and looked weak around people, but that's never stopped them from coming to me and telling me their problems...it's important to have that vulnerability.

Particularly with vulnerability being an uncommon or unaccepted characteristic in many professional settings, having a leader with the courage to display it has a profound effect on people.

Inspiration drawn from LGBTQ+ leaders' self-development spreads to those around them. The lessons of their stories can be applied to individuals navigating their development and overcoming obstacles, far beyond those on LGBTQ+ journeys. "We can make so many incremental changes, but at the end of the day, what is the goal? My leadership theory is making sure we do the best for all people, in whatever ways we can," said Jennifer L. Dane. "And that may start out small, but in the end, the goal is to make sure there's true leadership and true progress for everyone."

Many contributors described hearing the sentiment "If this leader can do *that thing*, then maybe I can accomplish *this thing*." LGBTQ+ stories can inspire anyone on a developmental journey.

CHAPTER 10

Everybody Transitions

As different as transgender experiences may seem from cisgender perspectives, transitions are fundamental human experiences. The changes and evolutions we move through are often the most important and impactful developmental catalysts for who we become as adults, as members of society, and as leaders. The stark, visible, and visceral nature of transition for transgender leaders illuminates those developmental impacts and can be examined for insights relevant to all leaders. With a deeper understanding of transition, leaders can support others during life transitions to leverage the challenge for the better, and help people thrive. Raffi Freedman-Gurspan described transition journeys: "We know what it's like to be different, but we also know what it is to be human. We all share that experience of suffering. In the Buddhist tradition that's where conversation begins, around understanding the human condition."

Transgender leaders' earned wisdom and nuanced interpretation of transition can build essential bridges from their life stories to our own. Rodrigo Heng-Lehtinen described the inherent humanity in a transition journey:

There is something really emotionally resonant about the idea of authenticity and being kind of lost and figuring it out. And then trying to build a life of one's own creation. Trying to do what feels right for you, even though there's not much of a roadmap for it and it's certainly not what anyone expected of you. That resonates with a lot of people...those kinds of themes are much more universal than just being trans. That's just trying to be human.

Leaders who acknowledge and embrace shared human experiences better serve every member of their team.

My Story, by Sabrina Bruce

We all have secret burdens. We have a book about our life that we write every single day. I only get to see chapters from people I work with, my friends, or family. Knowing my story led me to understand how other people are on similar journeys. They may not be dealing with something as big as transition or coming out, but their transition could be something like going from single to married or from no kids to having kids. I understand how those processes work for everybody; transition is not unique to transgender people. It helps me understand a lot of people have things going on. It's easy to think you're the center of the world. But realizing I fought this battle on my own for 25 years with barely anybody knowing makes me realize other people probably have similar things they're dealing with.

Before gender transition, I never really thought about how many transitions we go through. After transition, I looked back on my own life and realized I was full of transitions. The transition from high school to college, from civilian to military. Understanding that each of those had its own challenges helped me understand I'm not alone. When someone transitions from not having a kid, to having a kid, it's a scary experience. I can relate to the fear. I can't relate to having kids, I don't have any kids, but what I can relate to is that unknown, that fear. That realization helps me sit down with another and understand a little bit about what they're going through.

Upon graduating high school, I thought, "Man, what am I going to do now? Where does my life go?" It felt like my life was starting for the first time. I felt that feeling again after I began my transition. And so perhaps the same could be said for somebody who gets married to the love of their life and their life is starting fresh for the first time. Maybe we have those fresh starts each time. As members of the military, we go through a transition every two to four years when we go to a new base, a huge jump! When I stepped off the plane in Africa, my first time overseas, the air smelled different and all the sights and sounds around you are just vastly different than anything you've ever seen before.

Transgender people make sacrifices to be who we are. Those sacrifices could be family, friends, a stable job, or housing. But when you make those sacrifices, it's not necessarily a detriment to your life. It's a challenge! It adds to you and makes you who you are. It gives you a different experience, not one that's wrong. I hope if people read my story, they take away from it that my life was tough at times, but I'm a better person because of it. You don't necessarily get to see the gem underneath until you polish it, and transitioning was my polish. I hope people going through transitions can say the same for themselves.

I relate transition to other things in life because the transition is something people understand more than they think. When you think about somebody being transgender and you're a straight cisgender person, you might ask, "How do I relate? I've had no transitions in my life." Maybe they can read my story and think about how they have their own struggles and how they've dealt with transitions in their life because there are transitions we all deal with. It's a matter of framing and helping people to realize these events allow you to grow and don't necessarily hurt you.

My transition was my moment, my testing moment. I was put into the fire and had to either burn up or come out on the other side. A lot of people have similar moments.

Moving Past Expectations

For most people, adulthood involves navigating expectations and developing the capacity to establish their own path. In early adulthood, expectations of membership groups and social surroundings often shape people. The values, norms, and expectations of those groups build the foundational self, provide people their identity, and tell them how to navigate their lives. Meeting group standards becomes essential to an individual's sense of identity. Therefore, a primary driver becomes the need to seek external validation and harmony with others.

The evolution to a more self-directed and autonomous way

of being involves beginning to take objective perspectives on the standards and expectations of others. Adults who become more sophisticated in their way of understanding themselves begin to internally generate their standards. They focus on meeting their own expectations, while the expectations of others become additional information they may factor into the larger picture. Important others may be major characters in someone's story, but they no longer author it; instead the person writes their own.

Brooklyn Marquis explained how she became aware of societal gender constructs and the impact those expectations had:

> I grew up in male culture and saw all of this patriarchy. I contributed to it because I was constantly overcompensating for my lack of masculinity. I had to learn how to be this way. That's what I was told I needed to do. It's what I was brainwashed into thinking I needed to do to be a man in this world, or at least to pretend. I did a lot of acting and learning to be a man. Now, on the other side of this journey, I have an incredible perspective of how much I didn't know and how much I just went along with expectations of what it is to be male. It's been eye-opening.

Expectations carried from others are not only constrictive or unhealthy for people. Often they are optimistic and well-intended desires for individuals from those who care most about them, and even the hopes they created earlier in life. Sabrina Bruce spoke of navigating her early expectations:

> Being able to adjust your thinking ties heavily into coming out and transitioning. You have to switch gears. Sometimes not even gears, you have to switch the whole car. When you transition, you adjust all your hopes and dreams and all the

luggage that you've carried from your parents, all their hopes and dreams for you. You adjust all of that and switch it over to building new hopes and new dreams.

Becky Burke leverages her authenticity to support the young women she coaches. She said:

> When we say "people living their authentic lives," that could mean millions of different things. For me, it means being in a relationship, marrying a woman. There's so many things that young women deal with. "My parents are making me major in this and that's not who I am." So many different things you could put under that umbrella. Live your life the way that you want to live it. Date who you want to date. Major in whatever you want to major in.

Moving past expectations comes with fear and anxiety. People may worry they will lose their place, no longer belong, be ostracized, or even lose their very identity. Working to create a path in life is scary and painful for any adult; changes require courage. The willingness and ability to face that fear allow individuals to move through many of life's transitions while fortifying and strengthening them as people and as leaders.

Facing the Fear

Fear and anxiety during the destabilizing process of change can feel insurmountable; many people get held captive in their comfort zone. The wisdom and insight developed from facing fears can enable understanding of self and others and for authentically supporting change. One basic aspect of leadership is enabling others to engage in activities they may not on their own. Leaders who faced down their own fears of change are better prepared to support and empower others to do the same, even when people are inclined to resist or avoid the associated discomfort.

Jude Harris, senior vice president of production and development at media production company Gunpowder and Sky, translated the deeper insights she developed about people's natural insecurity to help them connect with their true self. She said:

> Transition was the scariest thing I've faced in my life. Facing it, and moving through it, and being forced to do it in a very public way, brought me an enormous amount of courage and knowledge about my own fear and other people's fear. When I'm encouraging risk taking or pushing people to connect with their truth, talent, and creative capabilities, it comes from a place of knowledge and authority I didn't have previously.

Behavioral health administrator and army sergeant Zaneford Alvarez' transition journey fortified his leadership: "The perspectives I have positively influenced my decision-making process on how to take care of soldiers... I'm grateful for my triumphs and tribulations because it's helped me to become a passionate leader." Drawing gratitude from challenges enables leaders to more readily apply the lessons of those challenges to future crucibles.

Similarly, Sabrina's facing down fear through transition enabled her to tackle the discomfort of taking on more demanding leadership roles:

> I knew I would have to do things out of my comfort zone... I took that leap of faith, because I knew I was prepared for the challenge. In fact, I was made for it. My transition, that burden I carried for so long, left me strong. I faced down my gender dysphoria and came out on top. I knew in my heart, if I could

face that, where my life was literally on the line, I could defi-
nitely face [this] down... My transition showed me I had more
mettle than I ever gave myself credit for. Every day I prove it
to myself and to a world that doubts my existence is valid.

Tapping into previous successes when facing fear or discomfort
is an important ingredient for tackling future challenges. Professional coaches and therapists frequently help clients overcome fear
of change by guiding them through the process of accessing prior
change successes and using those as fuel to tackle new challenges.

Danica Roem connected facing her fears to how she now
builds inclusive communities:

It's not just LGBTQ people coming out, it's a lot of people trying
to live what their truth is...we all have fears that live in our
mind about what will happen when we're spotted, what will
happen if someone were to know our reality. You realize how
much fear governs decision-making because you're trying to
not get yourself hurt either emotionally, mentally, or physically
for that matter... When you do confront it you can develop a
sense of empathy for other people going through their own
version of it. That's where you try to be as accommodating and
welcoming as possible.

Amanda Fisher described how she helps others facing their own
insecurities:

After transition, junior people would come by my office to chat
and eventually to seek career advice and mentorship. Most
of those people were women, people of color. There were
even a couple of white men. Most were not in my supervisory
chain of command. I found this surprising, because I didn't
feel anything in particular had changed about me, though in

retrospect of course, I had changed a great deal in how I presented outwardly and how people related to me. After a while, I asked a couple of these people what made them come by my office, and I heard almost the same response: *"Your transition displayed some visible vulnerability, and that made you approachable."* As a white male, where so much identity is built around concealing insecurity, I didn't anticipate how freeing it would be to shed that heavy coat.

Amanda's example shows how by facing one's own insecurity, leaders can better support and mentor others.

Fortifying the Self

With grit and confidence gained from overcoming fear of change, leaders are no longer captive to others' expectations and have new perspectives on themselves. As they enter new spaces, they enter with new strengths and capacities. Leaders can use forward momentum to write the next chapters of their story and refine the contours of themselves in that story. The journey gives them the chance to fortify their very identity. Transgender experiences show tremendous opportunities coming out of major life transitions. Leveraging changes provides the chance to own an identity and cultivate who an individual really wants to be. Commenting on her opportunity to do this, Sabrina Bruce said:

> Every time I see my name, I think *I picked that name.* The name is something special to me...it defines who I am. I get to reflect on my name. What does Sabrina mean? Who is that person? I had the chance to define every single aspect of Sabrina. Everything the world sees now is me. It's all been things I've picked.

Sabrina captured the power people can draw from writing even one aspect of their story and sharing it with the world.

Lorena Soto described this opportunity as occurring even in the midst of incredible challenges:

> Queer people sometimes do an internal inventory straight people might not have to. There's privilege in being accepted without question. When you're queer and you don't have that, the internal inventory you have to do actually makes you stronger. I see it all the time in my trans siblings, the courage it takes for them to be who they are.

While taking stock may be prompted by the need to survive in hostile environments, the intentionality of examining the self is powerful.

Louis Swanson shared his understanding of the things we all share, regardless of gender:

> Transition made me a better leader by showing me that, as humans, we are more alike than we are different. Female humans and male humans are not separate species. Transition simply made it easier for the public to see who I am and treat me accordingly, and for me to live an authentic, happy life. Contrary to assumptions, transition did not make me into a new or different person. I'm exactly the same person now as prior to transition. I am still an introvert. My opinions, attitudes, and preferences are exactly the same. Nothing has changed except how I'm viewed and treated by others, and my comfort with myself... The sole difference in my behavior is I now tend to be a bit more assertive. My opinions are treated as more valuable than they previously were, bolstering my courage to speak up. I realized I have the right to voice my concerns as much as anyone else.

Leaders' journeys through adulthood allow them to speak up for themselves with more confidence and less concern for others' expectations.

There is an evaluative process many transgender individuals engage as an opportunity to define the self. Sabrina Bruce said:

> You're forced to take a look at your life and evaluate it. Everything about you is under your own microscope lens. You're looking at your mannerisms and features. You're evaluating them. Do you want to keep them or put them by the side? That introspection leads to asking, "Hey, what do I like about myself? What makes me, me?" When I first transitioned, one of my friends put it plainly. He said, "*You have this opportunity to define your own life.*"

In re-making herself, Sabrina went beyond the changes fundamental to transition. She engaged in introspection about herself and got in touch with her full identity. This often difficult process of introspection contributes productively to leader development. "That [introspection] develops the courage, strength, and audacity you need to be a leader and to change the world," said Lorena. "That's what it got me. I am [bold] even when I am afraid. I'm not going to step down, I'm not going to be quiet, because I was for too long." The power and courage harnessed by facing down the world's expectations can be what forges a leader's strength to change the world.

Dominic Longo extends this concept by describing how queer flourishing provides a spark for all of us:

> The very word queer, the root meaning is *against the grain*. In some ways in this world where the Ho-Hum is the norm, all flourishing is queer. Yet it is our destiny. It's what we're

made for. I think truly all beings are made to flourish. And yet, somehow it goes against the grain of society to really flourish. I see how straight folks look at queer folks like, "My gosh those queer people have something I want. They're so fabulous. They're so courageous. They're so unfettered by these strictures"—which I do believe are maybe more imprisoning for straight people than for queer people. So that kind of attraction—part of the straight world looks to queer people with admiration. They can just write the story their own way. I think as queer people who are against the grain in terms of gender and sexual orientation, we have maybe more zigzag pathways that are inviting and unconventional by definition. That opens up new possibilities for everyone.

Given the need to flourish, and the prevalence of transitions in people's lives, how can leaders harness these lessons to help guide us? How can people be more intentional about making the best of transition experiences? What should individuals think about or deliberately reflect upon while going through an "against the grain" experience? How can leaders leverage crucible moments as developmental experiences? What can leaders do to assist their people?

Understanding leadership development opportunities arising from transition can help everyone tap into the value of their change experiences in life and leadership. While individuals may not always see themselves in the journey of transgender leaders, this genuinely human experience is universal. Metamorphosis is truly a story about all of us. Having examined lessons drawn from LGBTQ+ stories, we'll focus on how to apply them. In Part III we will learn how leaders can promote, foster, and leverage queer leadership superpowers.

Superpowers at Work

Practical Guidance for Leaders

CHAPTER 11

Leveraging Diversity

We can't say it enough—queer leadership capacities are particularly essential for addressing today's complex adaptive challenges. These challenges are emergent, unpredictable, boundaryless, and have unclear solutions and potentially even unknown end-states. For example, addressing diversity, equity, and inclusion (DEI) concerns can be understood as a complex adaptive challenge because there are rarely right answers and the ground upon which we understand DEI is frequently shifting. These issues, with intersecting and continuously changing variables such as human factors, societal trends, current events, historic norms, systemic inequities, and potentially catastrophic consequences, can be difficult to accurately identify, assess, navigate, and work toward acceptable and measurable solutions. Leadership professor Katherine Phillips, reviewing a decade's worth of research, stated, "If you want to build teams or organizations capable of innovating, you need diversity."[1] Acknowledging the considerable challenges, she said:

> Research has shown that social diversity in a group can cause discomfort, rougher interactions, a lack of trust, greater perceived interpersonal conflict, lower communication, less cohesion, more concern about disrespect, and other problems. So what's the upside? The fact is that if you want to build teams or

organizations capable of innovating, you need diversity. Diversity enhances creativity. It encourages the search for novel information and perspectives, leading to better decision-making and problem solving. Diversity can improve the bottom line of companies and lead to unfettered discoveries and breakthrough innovations. Even simply being exposed to diversity can change the way you think.[2]

Leaders at all levels need to translate diversity into success by working through the challenges and developing strategies of inclusion. With diverse teams, leaders need to absorb information from people, which requires active listening and the ability to integrate multiple perspectives.

Team sports show the value of diversity in achieving goals. How many games would an American football team with 22 punters win? How about a hockey team with six goalies? It seems absurd, but the point is clear. Without specialized skills and backgrounds from diversity, success is much harder to achieve. Patricia Rose believes diversity is one of the most potent tools in our arsenal. "When people in other countries see us working together across different races, genders, religions, and sexual orientations, it sends a powerful message about democracy," said Rose. "Diversity has always been our greatest strength as a nation and as a military. We know from experience when you tell the truth and live with integrity, that's better for everyone and makes your organization stronger."

The challenge for organizations is threefold. They must recognize diversity is not just an eye test, bring in diverse talents, and create a culture for diverse talent to flourish. For most people, the diversity around them is a fact, even if it takes work to understand the depth of it. For everyone, inclusion is an act. A powerful one everyone can take steps to enhance.

The Diversity Iceberg and Intersectionality

Think about the last meeting you attended or the big Zoom call you were on. How many aspects of diversity could you observe using only your eyes? Top of your mind are probably age, skin color, and gender expression. Interestingly, ask yourself if gender expression was on your list as sex, gender, or gender identity and consider if that's something you can know with visual information only! That's clearly not all the diversity in the room. Human diversity is very much the classic iceberg where 90 percent or more of the distinct qualities are not visible by scanning the surface.

Dr. Lorna Rodriguez gives us examples of the diversity we can't see, and describes the challenge and opportunity of intersectional identities.

I am queer, Latinx, I speak with an accent, and particularly when I'm tired it becomes very obvious English is not my first language. I am female by birth, but sometimes I look like a boy, and I'm even left-handed (not considered a gift when you are a surgeon). This intersectionality has helped me, though, because I usually don't know what the problem is when someone is struggling to respect me. I usually guess wrong.

When I learn what was really bothering them, I'm relieved, because in my mind I'm thinking, "Oh, that's the problem? I thought the problem was that I'm Puerto Rican." It helps me keep my sense of humor and my glass half-full perspective because it is usually just *one* of those things and not the others that are under attack—not all my wonderfully diverse features all at once. When I feel my other aspects are accepted by someone, I consider that a head start.

Sexual orientation, gender identity, language, and handedness are only a few examples of hidden diversity. While an exhaustive list would fill this book, it's worth pointing out more categories such as family status, socioeconomic status, religion, values, education, physical ability, nationality, neurodiversity, living arrangements, address, personality traits, risk tolerance, hobbies and interests, medical history, professional rank or title, and life experience. When considering these influences, you quickly realize the infinite combinations of diversity existent within humanity and how every individual has a unique, multi-faceted story. Two individuals who are both huge soccer fans probably won't have similar views when one is a wealthy, white, cisgender American, and the other is a queer, brown Brazilian of modest means. However, those shared interests can be points of building bridges and cohesive teams.

The LGBTQ+ community is heavily intersectional and very cognizant of those intersections, because sexual orientation and gender identity can be layered on top of every other identity. As Lorna experienced, when another identity of an LGBTQ+ person is also marginalized, challenges multiply. With the right circumstances, there can also be opportunity. To understand and help unlock their potential, a lot of listening is required. Many LGBTQ+ leaders honed their listening and observation skills to stay safe; leaders need to utilize those same skills to help those around them succeed.

Often, the first step to opening up listening is admitting you don't know everything. Jennifer L. Dane's experiences with her marginalized identities let her recognize the multiple-layer complexity others have and all the facets of identity where she wasn't knowledgeable. Leaders at all levels need to learn more about their people and ask them how they can move forward together. Jennifer explained that if she doesn't know those things, it's a lot harder to advocate for her folks.

Think about how perceptions shift when we treat others the way they want to be treated instead of the way we'd want to be treated. This is the upgrade from the "Golden Rule" to the "Platinum Rule." Treating others the way we'd like to be treated is like a reflex. It takes no effort but doesn't unlock the full potential of those around us. Treating folks the way they want to be treated takes work; it requires active engagement to listen and ask questions. Applying the Platinum Rule is essential to inclusion. Kimberly Morris put it this way: "There is strength in differences...the glue that holds it all together is treating someone like you value you them."

Even people working on diversity sometimes forget this. Lorena Soto conducted a training session on inclusivity and intersectionality for a group working in the LGBTQ+ community. Of all attendees, only two were people of color. Lorena led an exercise where she taught them about intersectionality and the need to acknowledge we all have a lot to learn in these spaces.

It was interesting to see how shocked they were as I did an exercise where I gave them cards telling them who they were. This is your race, your class, your documentation status, your HIV status, your gender identity. Then I started giving them scenarios. If you felt comfortable in this situation you took a step forward, if not you took a step back. By the time it was done, we had a conversation about what that meant. It was amazing to me that one woman raised her hand and said, "I don't think I should be in charge. I have no business being in charge of [this organization]. I'm in a mostly black community and I'm a white woman." I said, "Just the fact you said that, you realized that, makes me more comfortable you're in charge, because you acknowledge you probably don't have business being in charge here.

Raffi Freedman-Gurspan's intersectionality as a trans, Jewish adoptee and person of color drives and sustains her dedication to human rights work:

I see the discrimination and persecution these communities faced, yet there's this constant beat of a song saying, "we have to endure, we have to survive." That percolated up for me, looking at the long-term need and feeling dedicated and obligated to help kids like me and kids who weren't like me."

She emphasized the importance of acknowledging your role in a given space, particularly in advocacy work with diverse populations.

First is being very honest about your own truth. One of the things I'm always very aware of is where I don't have direct experience, but where I can be an ally. I believe that an ally is someone who stands up and speaks with a community, but doesn't do it on their behalf.

Bree was a panelist during a "Charm School," a class for newly promoted generals and civilian executives in the Air Force, to teach about engaging with minority groups. One general asked a question about the best way to engage with someone having negative experiences based around their identity. Another panelist recommended providing them with dignity and respect and to treat them the way the general would want to be treated. Interjecting,

Bree suggested the approach could be harmful. The other panelist was taken aback, but had an epiphany. Perhaps this general was someone who wanted to be pushed and challenged at every opportunity by her leadership, but the struggling individual wanted a supportive word or an ear to listen. The only way to know was to ask, to treat the individual the way they wanted to be treated. If leaders treat everyone the same, even if that's the way they prefer to be treated, they are explicitly saying to people that they don't see them for who they are. They fail to achieve inclusion.

Creating Cultures of Inclusion

Given there's a lot to be gained through diversity, how do organizations reap the benefits of diversity? It's incredibly important for leaders to understand that diversity without inclusion is insufficient. It takes deliberate inclusion to unlock the potential that diversity brings to organizations. Leaders must have the tools and mindset to create a culture of inclusion where everyone is enabled and empowered to contribute.

In 1968, British military strategist Liddell Hart wrote, "Vitality springs from diversity—which makes for real progress so long as there is mutual toleration, based on the recognition that worse may come from an attempt to suppress differences than from acceptance of them."[3] When Hart wrote, he wasn't discussing what is now somewhat accepted, if unevenly distributed, about the value of diversity within organizations. He was discussing how to deliver improved peace following conflict through discussion between allies with differing views. His argument is similar to how diversity of thought and experience brings value to our organizations today: better choices and better results.

Yet, Hart set the bar too low. He argued that when you tolerate diversity you do better than fighting against it. Instead, when you celebrate diversity, and make inclusion a purposeful part of a leadership philosophy, you reach heights far greater than you would with mere toleration. Retired Air Force lieutenant general Christopher Miller puts it this way: "inclusion with diversity is powerful, but diversity without inclusion fosters division."[4] Phillips relates the pain associated with diversity and inclusion work to the pain of exercise. You may not want to do it, but you'll be better for it.

Leaders must move beyond toleration of differences implied by having non-discrimination policies or treating everyone with a modicum of dignity and respect. To achieve a culture of inclusion, leaders must:

- be willing to learn
- set the standard
- explain your why
- call in contributions
- reflect and reevaluate.

Be Willing to Learn

Since you're reading this book, you probably have a willingness to learn. Almost 60 percent of American adults read five or fewer books per year, and almost 20 percent read none![5] Willingness to read is a great start on willingness to learn. We have described the developmental journeys of LGBTQ+ individuals, but don't stop there. We've included a list of additional resources in the Further Reading section at the end of the book to continue your journey if you want to keep reading.

One area anyone can learn more about is being an ally. Jeannie Gainsburg, author of *The Savvy Ally*, an outstanding primer on allyship to the LGBTQ+ community, defines an ally as "a person who is not a part of a particular marginalized group but who stands up for and advocates for the rights of people in that group."[6] Advocating for people starts with learning. If you can't understand where they've been and what they need to succeed, how can you make their case to others?

Jennifer Brown made the case for this learning mindset and connected it to inclusive leadership. "To be a leader in today's ever-changing landscape requires learning, reflection, and most importantly, altering old habits and mindsets."[7] Leaders must learn the stories of the people they lead. Learn where they've been, who they are, and where they want to go. Learn what obstacles are still in their path. Use that knowledge to alter how they relate with people and how their behaviors might change and grow.

In 2015, after four years and several deployments, where he was in the first cohort of women to ever serve aboard submarines, Blake Dremann was transferred to the Pentagon. While there, he began his transition despite military regulations prohibiting it. He took a huge risk to be his best self and was scared to death that someone would notice something about him was off. Maybe they'd pick up on his short hair, his deepening voice, or perhaps the way he carried himself. He thought he didn't want a boss who would learn or pick up on any of these things. He thought it would be safer to go unnoticed. He was completely wrong.

> My new boss was everything I was scared would happen. She was a woman. She was Army. She was a lieutenant colonel. She was smart. She noticed me. She pulled me aside on my third day and was asking questions. She asked where I was living. She asked about my family. Then she leaned in close and asked me if I used a different name outside of work. I froze.

My stomach was in my chest. I'm pretty sure my face turned a bright red, making it impossible to lie. This was the do or die moment. I took a deep breath and said I use Blake when not at work. I was going to change it legally but not until after my clearance renewal had been completed, so my birth name was just fine. We talked a few more minutes and then she sent me home. About 30 minutes after I got home, I got a phone call from her. She said she had discussed my name with the team, and if I was okay with it, they would like to call me Blake. She said, we'll use it like a call sign. Of course I agreed and you would not have been able to knock that smile off my face for the rest of the day if you tried.

Dr. Nicholas Grant, president of GLMA: Health Professionals Advancing LGBTQ Equality, said his best boss always wanted to know more, and to know about him personally. He described her as very intentional in her mentorship and "exceptionally skilled at checking in on me as a person." Nick's boss, an ally, got to know him so she could advocate for him. She was a perfect example for how Jeannie Gainsburg thought of allies. Jeannie wrote, "the more we learn about LGBTQ+ individuals and communities, the better we become at changing hearts and minds outside those communities. We can help bridge the gap between these two worlds and aid in understanding and communication."[8]

Further, the more leaders learn about their colleagues, the more they'll identify their unique inputs, which can be leveraged. Russ Houser described the value of being different:

For me, the queer superpower was realizing from a very early age that I was different. And then learning how to leverage that. If I wasn't going to be better than my peers, then I was going to be different. Different is good and I was going to own that. Difference is what got me doing things that other people might not do. Different became my leveraged superpower.

A willingness to expand perspectives and see more than one side of a story can also be hugely important in a learning journey. In the case of developing LGBTQ+ leaders, it's being able to reframe the challenging experiences they've faced as development opportunities. It's not about feeling sorry for them, but about creating the opportunity for growth. Jude Harris said she "encourages all leaders not just to look at the trauma and hardship [of minority journeys], but to explore the unique strengths that trans and other LGBTQ+ and BIPOC people have." While leaders must understand the difficulties, if they focus only on trauma and hardship, it's easy to get stuck in the past instead of looking to the future.

Set the Standard

People expect leaders to lead, and it is often the example leaders set that individuals think of as leadership. But let's clear one thing up first: setting the standard is not about being the best. It is not about being the smartest, the technical expert, or the fastest to accomplish a task. Setting the standard is about attitude, values, and mindset. So how do leaders model inclusive standards?

Amanda Fisher recounts one way an inclusive leader set the standard for her environment:

My boss, who learned I was transgender three days before I reported, stabbed a pen through the air individually at each department head in the organization at a staff meeting the day before I arrived, and growled, "Her name is Amanda Fisher, she is a woman, and there WILL NOT be a problem. She will feel welcome, and she is a part of my team. DO NOT fuck this up, or I WILL END YOU." Sometimes an encouraging word is all it takes. The staff was very welcoming, and after I did my part and they got to know me and see that me being trans is not that big a deal, we've become great friends and shipmates. The message was clear. The standard is a welcoming environment of inclusion.

Setting the standard with the right attitude, values, and mindset means it's more than words communicating the standard to others. Words may frame the conversation, but meaning is conveyed by action. A simple example is someone telling their staff they all must do their part to keep the facility clean...then walking right past a piece of trash on the floor. Issues walked past or ignored set the standard that those things don't matter, regardless of what may have been said. In LGBTQ+ contexts, one of the most damaging things a leader can do is ignore, or worse yet, encourage, derogatory language or actions. When homophobic or misogynistic jokes are told in the workplace and the leader overhears and doesn't do anything, the standard has been set: it's okay to use that language even if the organization's policy is non-discrimination. Leaving it to others to decide if they're hurt enough by the language to report it is not an option. Individuals may not feel safe enough to do so, particularly if they've just seen someone above them walk by the issue. Setting the standard means living up to the ideals leaders and organizations espouse when it comes to inclusion and enforcing them with others.

Inclusive leaders also need to be okay with not having all the answers, a willingness to admit errors, and an openness to connection. If that sounds a bit like how we discussed the value of vulnerability earlier, you're right! A leader who tries to set a superhuman standard where everything must be perfect at all times is setting themselves and their organization up for failure.

Explain Your Why

Simon Sinek's book *Start with Why* is a modern leadership classic and, as of June 2023, his TEDx talk on the subject has over 62 million views. Sinek argues that having a reason why we do things is what drives us to success, not what we do or how we do it. He said, "People don't buy what you do; they buy why you do it. If you talk about what you believe, you will attract those who believe what you believe."[9] In the context of inclusion, a leader's *why* is vital to others buying into the culture you want to create and is not something to keep to yourself. Paired with setting the standard, it provides a powerful example of both motivation and follow-through to create inclusive environments.

Personal reasons why inclusion matters can be just about anything but they have to be genuine. We explored the value of authenticity and the downsides of being inauthentic, which also applies to expressed motivation. Doing inclusion for the sake of not looking bad, following trends, or because you were told to do so won't cut it. For each of us, there's probably at least one reason to be inclusive that resonates.

For some people, the primary *why* for inclusion is economic. In *The Economic Case for* LGBT *Equality,* Professor M. V. Lee Badget investigates the topic from individual to national levels. She says, "there is now a lot of evidence from different angles that all fits the idea that more inclusion leads to increases in GDP per capita."[10] Her work shows LGBTQ+ exclusionary policies prevent individuals from living up to their potential and can cost a nation more than 1 percent of their gross domestic product. This statistic solely reflects inclusion based on sexual orientation and gender identity. When other historically marginalized groups are also included the effects multiply. If an organization requires profit to succeed, the economic case is a powerful *why*.

Optimization imperatives are other reasons leaders create inclusive environments. If an organization needs to find the best solutions to any given challenge, optimization is one *why* to choose. There is ample evidence supporting inclusion as a key factor in creating stronger solutions. Research shows inclusive teams make better business decisions up to 87 percent of the time and teams using inclusive processes make decisions twice as fast.[11] Studies also show that inclusivity augments other factors that are preconditions for better solutions, such as increased sense of belonging, higher levels of trust, and increased employee engagement.[12] Creating solutions derived from the integration of multiple perspectives is another powerful *why*.

A third common *why* leaders may identify with is ideals based. Whether they believe inclusion is important based on principles, past experiences, or morality, they think it's the right thing to do. This inner sense of what's right may be understood and experienced differently from different cognitive-developmental levels. For example, in the socialized stage, inclusion may be important as the societally appropriate thing to do. At the self-authored stage, it may stem from an internal moral compass or sense of what's appropriate despite societal or cultural views that may oppose some forms of inclusion. Stanley Masczak said:

> Make connecting, learning, and growing priorities, not for inclusion's sake alone, but with the understanding that these skills are what make us more innovative, successful organizations full of outside-the-box thinkers who are less likely to go

with the status quo, and more likely to do what's right in the face of adversity, or see the solution no one else can because they're stuck in negative groupthink.

Regardless of the reason, leaders who explain why they believe inclusion is important can engage with the people they lead in a manner that secures buy-in, taps into potential, and helps navigate complexity and change.

Call in Contributions

No matter how welcoming an environment is, some people are uncomfortable engaging even when they have valuable contributions to make. Having already set the standard that it's acceptable to not always have the answers, calling in contributions is where leaders actively pull people into the conversation or solution-creation process.

Dayna Walker calls in contribution frequently. She watches for:

the quiet, reserved person sitting quietly in the corner who may never get to express their opinion because nobody bothers to ask them, who don't feel they're a contributor. Many times, I've sat in conference rooms and watched two or three people talk in a room of 20. I'd pick out those I know can probably contribute, give them an opportunity to speak, and say, "Hey, what do you think?" It gives them a voice where they otherwise would have been passed over.

When calling in contribution, think about language. Most people have been in rooms where a leader goes around asking if anyone has anything to add, or points and says, "Anything from you?"

Heads shake or a quick no is often the response. But if the leader does what Dayna did and asks an open-ended question that can't have a simple yes or no answer, they're far more likely to draw people into the conversation. Questions starting with how, what, or why are best at bringing people into the discussion. These questions also make the query feel more like open dialogue, instead of quizzing, which can ease the minds of contributors that they're not being put on the spot.

Another useful practice for leaders is the concept of a warm call. This gives someone extra time versus a cold call requiring instant response. A leader might say, "I see Alex and Jamie both have something to add. Let's take those inputs, and then Liam, I'd like to hear your insights next." A warm call provides someone who may be hesitant to speak with advance warning, a clear opening, and time to prepare. It also messages to the individual, and the entire group, that the leader values their input. If leaders have set an inclusive environment where people are asked for input and aren't afraid to make mistakes, they're even more likely to get constructive feedback and contributions driving the conversation forward.

Reflect and Reevaluate

Charging ahead to drive inclusion while wearing blinders can be dangerous. There may be people hurt or feeling left out that we don't even notice. They're called blind spots because individuals can't see it themselves, at least without a bit of effort. Leaders need to slow down at times to reflect on what they are doing and understand what's happening around them. If it's not going well, consider course changes. Even if efforts at inclusion are paying dividends, consider what else might improve outcomes. Are there still systemic barriers in place to remove? In the *Journal of*

Character and Leadership Development, Christopher Miller wrote a series of questions leaders should consider as they evaluate their inclusion efforts.

> A leader of character can gauge how inclusive they and their organizations are by asking some simple questions, every day: Do I really listen to my people, and respect what they say whether or not I agree? Do I do so without prejudging their inputs and work based on a pre-existing expectation? Do I model, and see, indications of consistent respect between peers, and between leaders and followers? Do I allow disrespect to exist without correcting it? Are there in- and outgroups? Do I solicit, mentor, recognize and reward excellence and collaborative effort, and do I reject self-centered or prejudiced conduct whenever it becomes apparent? And finally, do I seek to give opportunities to people who bring diversity to the table in race, gender, background, culture, life experience, and cognitive style?[13]

Answers to these questions shine a light on where there's more work to be done.

How LGBTQ+ Leaders Leverage Diversity

While anyone can develop the ability to understand diversity and develop inclusive cultures, LGBTQ+ leaders' developmental journeys position them to do so almost automatically. Of course there are outliers, often seen among members of the community with more societal privilege or who had fewer crucible moments, but many LGBTQ+ journeys create an outward focus all about taking care of others.

While LGBTQ+ leaders may have better capacity for

perspective-taking because they've experienced situations from multiple different vantage points, they seem to value diverse viewpoints of others even more. Rather than say, "I am good at seeing the different perspectives myself, so I don't actually need others involved," these leaders are likely to seek out and be inclusive of additional voices because they understand the value in diversity of thought, and because they know what's left on the table when people overlook marginalized voices.

While teaching leadership at the US Naval Academy, Kris Moore worked to impart this knowledge to his midshipmen. Earlier, Kris explained how diversity and multiple perspectives can drive better solutions. Here he reveals how he tries to deliberately bring in additional perspectives.

> Let's say we're picking a planning team. When we're picking that team, maybe don't pick the first person that comes to mind. Sometimes the first person is going to be that white guy, because we're still early in our inclusion era. We need to stop and say, "How about this individual? They haven't had a chance to get one of these leadership positions and get the eyes of [senior leaders] on them and get that exposure. Why not them?"

The response Kris often heard was "Oh, well, they haven't done anything like that before." But there has to be a first time; leaders who provide opportunities create deliberate leadership development. LGBTQ+ leaders like Kris deliberately identify barriers holding people back and look to overcome them. Often, tackling diversity and inclusion issues comes first.

Lorena Soto tackled many of these issues when she became president of her local chapter of PFLAG, an organization that supports, educates, and advocates for LGBTQ+ people and those who love them.[14]

I took on diversity and inclusion and asked why there are only white people at these meetings when we're 86 percent Hispanic. Why aren't we reaching out to other people? Why is my queer community run by gay white men? Where are the women? Where are the minorities? Why isn't anybody being heard? I really started to push for change and diversity. I wanted people of all walks of life on my board.

She also went after the issue Kris identified of people not getting initial opportunities. She worked with soldiers who were leaving the military and told them "You don't have to be 100 percent qualified for a position. You have to be 60 percent qualified and smart." Lorena took her own advice and was hired as a field coordinator and immigration policy strategist for the ACLU (American Civil Liberties Union), where she has an even greater impact helping others.

Nick Grant and Liam Connors Smith both connected their leadership to developmental challenges they faced in the past. Nick leads with a lens on equity and an inclusive focus on the team. He credits his focus, and that of many others who faced marginalization, to a realization about the impacts of discriminatory behavior. Liam feels satisfaction being able to mentor and guide others on similar paths. He said, "I can use my own experiences to make [the organizational environment] more inclusive and all around more welcoming, just by being my authentic self."

Asked how her development journey shaped her, Lindsey Medina pointed to increased empathy and inclusivity, particularly for people who struggle to connect in easily identifiable ways. So her first priority when new people come to work for her is figuring out how to make a connection. She won't take initial appearances or superficial dismissal for granted.

You have to keep pursuing [connection], especially as a supervisor, to know your people and to listen to what they're actually saying. Maybe he doesn't have much to say, but he still wants to be invited, or he takes a long time to warm up to people, but you can't just say, "then I'm not going to bring him to the table." When they're comfortable, and they feel safe, they're going to open up, they're going to start connecting with you.

You have to provide an environment where people feel comfortable, feel like they can trust you enough to talk with you about their family, or to talk with you about stuff they're struggling with. My journey made me pretty good at being able to set people at ease in a new environment so that they can blossom, be who they are, and contribute in their own way.

CHAPTER 12

Opening Doors and Supporting Growth

How can leaders tear down barriers still standing in the way of LGBTQ+ individuals? Further, how can they actively open doors and set conditions in their teams and organizations supporting continued growth? We start with how leaders can prepare themselves to do this work and then move into ideas that can be incorporated into leadership and organizational efforts. Leaders, supervisors, or colleagues of LGBTQ+ employees can also utilize the information from Part II to serve as allies and advocates and to create better workplaces.

Prepare to Work

An important criterion for doing this work is understanding it takes effort. Change does not occur without active, deliberate work, especially by leaders. Begin by taking stock of your readiness to be a change agent. Being an ally and advocate is not simply a state of being, it is an action and influence-oriented presence for positive change. Lorena Soto described some of the challenges she faced trying to help organizations do better:

I've dealt with management who've said, "Oh my God, so do we have to cater to everybody?" If you want to be successful, yeah you do. Because morale in the workplace is tied to productivity. If you want to be productive, yes, you need to be able to have those conversations. You need to have training. You need to celebrate Pride. You need to put in the steps.

Once leaders are ready to do the work, they should first look inside themselves. While we strive to provide examples all leaders can utilize to better support LGBTQ+ colleagues, it's important to consider who is doing this work. Leaders should understand what tools they have at their disposal, the conditions of their context, and more fundamentally, how they show up in this work. We ask you to think about yourself and the implications of what you bring to the table. During the research for this book, we asked many of our contributors: *Why did you choose to participate in this project?* We ask you to consider why you chose to read this book. Engaging in this self-analysis sets the conditions for authenticity and fortifies your work to lead change.

Self-Awareness

Self-awareness is an essential precondition for leaders aiming to create positive environments for LGBTQ+ colleagues. It's also an important quality for leaders to understand and manage how their reputation and others' perceptions of them may impact their leadership. Truly self-aware leaders are also inherently other-aware. Self-awareness is not solely about looking in the mirror and seeing yourself more clearly, it's also the ability to understand how others see you. An internal sense of self is truly understood only by you; reputation is understood and believed by others. Personal intentions are also only understood by you; perception is the reality others live in and respond to, so leaders must have clarity on what people around them are observing and assuming.

Leaders aware of their reputation and others' perceptions are better able to communicate with and influence people. Given that followers closely observe leadership by example, authentic behaviors, and whether the leader exhibits a say–do mismatch, leaders who hope to act as allies and set positive and empowering conditions for LGBTQ+ employees must be acutely aware of how they exemplify these values. What messages do words, actions, and behaviors send to perceptive LGBTQ+ colleagues? What messages are sent to all employees about acceptable and expected support of LGBTQ+ colleagues? Does the leader provide a visible and consistent example to be followed?

Stanley Masczak reflected on his privilege, stating:

As a white person who presents male, I become more aware of my privilege every day, and have increasing respect for those who have additional challenges and roadblocks I don't have. I know how exhausting it can be from my own lived experience and place of privilege; when I see others who have additional intersections leading powerfully and setting the example, it is much more inspiring and humbling.

The willingness to acknowledge privilege and understand how experiences differ as a result of privilege is an example of how self-awareness enables better leadership. Self-awareness is a first step in enabling the other-focused leadership that leaders should extend to all team members. It brings tangible benefits toward helping people thrive and getting their best performance. Because they are also other-aware, self-aware leaders identify the strengths of others and keenly employ those combined strengths toward mission success.

Enhanced self-awareness and a willingness to acknowledge their own shortcomings can help leaders better leverage diversity. Self-aware leaders know their strengths and weaknesses. They identify their gaps and surround themselves with resources and people that fill those gaps effectively. They understand, appreciate, *and* know how to leverage diverse perspectives, backgrounds, skills, and strengths. They actively seek out and utilize the least represented perspectives that would otherwise go unstated. They are more inclusive and draw more value out of inclusivity. Research in psychology, management, and economics shows that non-homogeneous teams have a variety of improved outcomes, likely because working with people who are different challenges our brains to break out of stale ways of thinking.[1] Self-aware leaders know working with people who all think the same might be efficient and comfortable, but working with people who think differently will be effective and foster personal growth and team development.

Acknowledging Bias

One of the most challenging aspects of self-awareness is willingness to acknowledge bias. A leader may assume being an ally or advocate means they are free of bias or above being influenced by stereotypes, societal norms, or stigma. But this narrow conception of ourselves is naive and not reflective of the nuance and complexity of the human mind. Bias is a foundational part of human thinking because it is biological. The brain was built for survival. When humans need to make fast decisions, such as fight or flight to avoid danger, they need information-processing shortcuts. The option chosen probably worked the last time the situation occurred, so cognitive bias helped keep people alive and therefore became hardwired.[2] It may also arise from the culture we consume, particularly in our formative years. Consider what surrounded you as you grew up consuming media and culture. Who were the frequent villains or criminals on TV? How did that shape your conscious or unconscious bias toward that group?

The study of social cognition examines how social forces shape how we think and act. In particular, research indicates that stereotyping is a tool people use to accomplish their goals, such as feeling in control, or the ability to understand and predict events. According to psychology researcher Gordon Moskowitz, people are inherently biased because all human thought and action is always in the service of the goals we have. He says, "These goals may be invisible to the naked eye, implicit (unconscious). But we are always pursuing a goal with every action, with every thought. Thus every action and thought is biased by these goals."[3] Research in social cognition has produced the concept of implicit bias, with results indicating that bias is socially constructed within our environments, and that we as individuals may lack awareness of our socially guided attitudes and stereotypes.[4]

With the adversity, marginalization, and stigmatization still faced by LGBTQ+ individuals, leaders must recognize how the prevalence of bias, prejudice, and hate all around them may have influenced their thinking. Over a long period of time, history, culture, science, politics, and religion "intertwined to create social discrimination" against the LGBTQ+ community, and a leader's embeddedness in these various domains has an impact on the forming of biases and entrenched ways of thinking.[5] Unexamined or unacknowledged, these may remain unconscious but impactful on efforts to support LGBTQ+ colleagues.

It's also important to remember that biases can include positive conceptions. If you picked up this book, you may have done so because of a positive bias toward the leadership skills of LGBTQ+ individuals. The authors' bias is on the front cover. But while well-intended, if these biases remain unexamined, what unhelpful impacts might our beliefs have? Could we unintentionally send the message that some level of adversity faced by LGBTQ+ leaders is useful, and therefore to some extent acceptable? Might we inadvertently come across as apologists for beliefs or actions that marginalize? Do we run the risk of over-simplifying the narrative to the point where the need to do better gets lost?

Even positive intentions, if enacted thoughtlessly, can be part of the problem. For example, a mentor who considers themselves an ally may be excited about the leadership potential they see in an LGBTQ+ mentee. They may encourage them to take on a new challenge, focusing on the developmental opportunity framed through their belief in the person's ability. But their positive bias may result in failing to notice or fully appreciate the threats of a non-inclusive environment, potentially pushing the mentee not just out of a comfort zone, but into a danger zone.

Leaders unwilling or unable to do the challenging and uncomfortable work of examining and addressing their own biases may do LGBTQ+ colleagues a disservice. Further, they miss opportunities to provide examples and lead the way for others to address their own biases. Through their vulnerability and openness, leaders can model the tough, but necessary work of honest self-awareness, self-assessment, and continuous striving to be better. Leaders owe this to their LGBTQ+ colleagues who are standing by ready to help.

Acknowledging Identity

Further educating themselves on LGBTQ+ identities and other key aspects of their experience is another worthwhile step for leaders. Additionally, reflecting upon one's identity is an important process. How do you think about, talk about, and present your own identity and what are the implications for your leadership? Would being more aware of those implications help you better appreciate the experiences of others?

For LGBTQ+ leaders working to set conditions for LGBTQ+ colleagues, how does identity play a role? How does their self-awareness, authenticity, and story sharing influence other people, the team, and the organization? Our contributors shared their stories to pave the way for others and described how certain dynamics changed before and after coming out or transitioning. Particularly interesting were those who experienced significant changes in their privilege. "It wasn't until I transitioned, and started presenting as a man, and experiencing society as a man, that I realized, 'Holy crap! Women are not treated the same as men,'" said Kris Moore, noting how differently men were responded to. "Reflecting on those experiences allowed me to hopefully treat people better and to voice my concerns when I see other people being treated differently in life."

For non-LGBTQ+ leaders, what role does identity play? How have they considered and explored their identity, if at all? How does their external display of identity impact their leadership, allyship, and advocacy? What does it take to engage in this work with true authenticity? How can non-LGBTQ+ leaders navigate their own privilege?

As Melissa Gumbs pointed out, often LGBTQ+ individuals are expected to do the work, but, especially in the face of marginalizing messages, allyship needs to arise from "people who are not directly impacted by this type of speech; it needs to be cis-het people that say something." Given an ally's privilege, what is the nature of their role, the potential for their impact, responsibility, and obligation? These questions illuminate the necessity for the self-awareness and self-work that enable honest and genuine allyship and advocacy.

Communicating

Some of the most important elements in creating safe spaces are how leaders communicate, the language they use, how they engage with LGBTQ+ colleagues, and importantly, that leaders *are* actively communicating. A basic pitfall for any leader to avoid is being a silent bystander. Leaders have a responsibility to speak up and take action to remove and prevent barriers to LGBTQ+ people thriving in the workplace. "If you're in a conversation with someone and they make a remark that's inappropriate, you as a non-LGBTQ+ person need to call it out and tell them it's not appropriate, as anyone would a slur based on racial stereotypes," said Blake Dremman straightforwardly. "We should do the same thing for LGBTQ+ stereotypes." Leaders, and all members of an organization, must become comfortable calling out unacceptable comments and behaviors and making the message clear to the entire team.

Sybil Taunton said that when she saw silence from leaders:

My empathic leadership style paired with my personal experiences facing adversity enabled me to take on difficult leadership challenges like supporting my team through the Black Lives Matter movement. I have never been more disappointed in the lack of solid leadership above and around me than I was during those critical months [after the death of George Floyd].

Leaders that couldn't personally identify with the movement froze and chose to do nothing, rather than acknowledging that leadership is also about supporting and listening, and that was the time to do so.

Communication is one of the most obvious and available tools non-LGBTQ+ leaders have at their disposal to support LGBTQ+ colleagues. "Leaders need honest, vulnerable communication," said Lorena Soto. "Let your staff know they can come to you about anything." Lorna Rodriguez added:

> If you're not queer, I invite you to do something, even if it is to engage in a conversation with someone you know who is. Ask them to share their stories about when they ran up against open prejudice and how they coped. Assure them that next time, you will be there to listen, comfort (if needed), and strategize a better path forward. There is nothing like new allegiances from diverse and unusual backgrounds to fire up a movement toward deliberate and conscious inclusion.

Leaders who don't speak or act to create the right conditions for LGBTQ+ colleagues are allowing stereotyping, marginalization, and even hatred to occur. Speaking up, and being conscious of how we talk and the messages our words convey, is essential for creating safe environments. Lorena describes the dangers of not having psychological safety in organizational environments.

> Before anything else [LGBTQ+ people] have to feel safe in their environment. People don't realize how important that is and how easy it is to make queer folk feel unsafe. When I do allyship training, I tell corporations and businesses, "You need to change how you talk." Our small talk in America is very personal. Hey, so are you married? How many kids do you

have? That doesn't sound threatening, but it does to a queer person. Because a queer person has to come out every single time they start a new job, meet a new person. I've been at jobs not even three days before I hear a gay joke. That right there tells me I am not safe. Of course, I'm not going to thrive in that environment, I can't thrive in that environment. I'm going to stay quiet and I'm going to stay down in that environment.

Using inclusive language is important to create LGBTQ+ safe environments. Lorena Soto highlighted how certain common terminology can be problematic:

A supervisor might do something they don't think is wrong, like saying, "Hey guys and girls." I hate being called a girl. I hate it. Something as simple as that can make a queer person uncomfortable, and that queer person isn't going to go to their boss and tell them that. There needs to be a person who makes sure they're training management on why it's so important to be inclusive.

Kristen Pecua, a lesbian satellite operator in the Space Force, shared how one of her mentors did this. "During our mentorship session, the little things like her asking if I had a spouse or partner rather than husband or boyfriend. It made me feel like I was part of a team." Good leaders take the time to educate themselves on inclusive language, monitor their speech, and understand how words might be received. If they don't know, they ask. LGBTQ+ leaders are willingly there to answer these questions.

One caution about asking individuals something about themselves or their minority group: it shouldn't be done simply to satisfy curiosity. If you're curious, google it. There's no need to place the burden on someone who has probably defensively answered similar questions before to explain it. However, if that conversation is used to build connection and enhance your ability to support, frame the discussion that way! Approach someone to support them or build a better relationship with them. That's what good leaders do!

Mentoring and Empowering

LGBTQ+ leaders speak often about efforts to empower and mentor LGBTQ+ colleagues. Sharing personal examples of what leaders did well, and not so well, in setting conditions for their own development can help other leaders to create conditions that enable and empower LGBTQ+ colleagues.

Explore the stories of LGBTQ+ leaders to avoid pitfalls and also to better understand, promote, and leverage their superpowers. Leaders should pay close attention to LGBTQ+ challenges in the workplace. Kris Moore spoke about being cognizant of adverse experiences that might be occurring, even when the individual may not be able to speak up for themselves. A leader can ask themselves "Am I seeing the full picture or is this individual being treated in a way they shouldn't be treated and they're not speaking up because they feel like they're going to be ostracized for speaking up?" Perhaps that individual can't share the full picture, but maybe someone else around them can. Identifying and promptly correcting unacceptable treatment is essential for making the workplace safe.

Alison Cruise talked about examining the environment for potential adversity:

My identity as a woman, and as a gay woman, intersect as I feel my positionality every time I walk into a room. It's almost like feeling as if you have two strikes against you. Two ways in which I'm really different from the majority of my white, straight, male counterparts in this heteronormative environment. I struggle with feeling dismissed or ignored sometimes. This feeling is way less now than it has ever been, but I'm cognizant we all develop at different rates and I always look around the room to try and imagine who else is feeling like they have strikes against them, what they are, and how this is playing out in their interactions. Taking it a step farther, we should try and understand those real or perceived inequities and work to validate the diversity in the room. What once felt like ways in which I lacked value in a conversation now feels like I have so much to add to the conversation. We cannot assume people get to this place on their own, and we need to actively engage in inclusion if we really want to celebrate diversity.

Alison's example highlights why leaders must be cognizant of how the environment may be exacerbating the experience of being in the minority and work deliberately to counteract those concerns through active inclusion.

Further, leaders must empower LGBTQ+ colleagues by backing their words with concrete and sustained actions. Jess Warren said that leaders must:

create spaces that say, "Anyone has a seat at this table. All voices matter. All identities matter. And you can be anyone, and still make a great impact here." Then back that up by ensuring individuals with diverse identity intersections have the same opportunities and get the same support in performance reviews for their work that cis, hetero, white folks do. THEN promote them! Promote people of diverse identities into senior roles to ensure you are driving the creation of inclusive products and organizations so that more talented, brilliant, diverse individuals want to join and stay in your organization.

Leaders should be conscious of how they invest in the development of their people, and look closely at how development opportunities are being allocated.

LGBTQ+ heightened self-awareness also helps them understand their own development needs. Mentors should be aware of this skill and approach conversations to leverage that ability. Blake Dremann explained:

> We bring to the forefront what we're good at, and where we may need to improve. That helps us have those conversations with our mentors honestly; they don't need to bring it out of us. There's no digging, there's no looking. It's already there. That's a big plus on our end. It makes it a little bit less difficult to have mentoring relationships.

He says mentors can take advantage of this opportunity by "helping people realize where their strengths lie and then letting them fly." Mentoring LGBTQ+ people is often an exercise in coaching, where the mentor is listening and asking questions to draw answers out of individuals while giving them the confidence to act upon their own ideas.

Blake continued describing how mentors can best serve LGBTQ+ mentees. "Know what to pay attention to, pay attention to how you speak to people, and how people speak to you." He explained that great mentors and leaders let people be themselves, give them flexibility, and focus on their ability to do the job and be a leader. It's important the mentee have the space to discuss issues related to their LGBTQ+ status when and how they see fit.

Raffi Freedman-Gurspan talked about experiences of being the first transgender person in a working environment:

> I wanted them to meet Raffi. Not the transgender staffer. Not the stereotype. I wanted them to meet me and I wanted them to understand I was here to do the work. A transgender woman is more than just that. They are a woman with spirit, character, intellect, interests, and humor.

Mentees should have the opportunity to focus on whatever they feel is most important and identify for themselves where they need or want mentor support.

This perspective aligns with expert guidance on enhancing inclusivity by communicating with affected individuals. A 2020 *Harvard Business Review* article on creating trans-inclusive workplaces suggested trans employees should be asked whether they prefer to speak up for themselves and whether they want to be present in inclusivity training. The authors say, "The simple act of consulting before taking action gives a trans person agency and autonomy in deciding how the situation should be handled."[6]

It's important for leaders to understand that when an LGBTQ+ colleague's status is playing an active role in their professional life they may face additional burdens beyond the potential negative experiences. Several contributors described how they have become safe confidants, mentors, and sources of support for other colleagues, both LGBTQ+ and not. If you have subordinate LGBTQ+ leaders, realize that they might be taking on others' challenges and emotional burdens. They need the time, space, and resources to manage that additional work. Further, they may need someone to talk with so they have the opportunity to process what they're carrying. We do a disservice to these individuals if we don't acknowledge and address the implied collateral duties of being authentic in the workplace.

With heightened understanding, leaders can help LGBTQ+ colleagues grow by understanding the challenges of their journey. Sabrina Bruce said, "When I accepted I was transgender, I was forced to pull that 'band-aid' off and expose part of myself to the world." Leaders who are willing to learn about both the hardships and the victories of a person's journey help treat wounds that may still be festering and enable healing as they come out and live openly in their workplace.

Mentors and leaders should be deliberate about setting conditions to help LGBTQ+ colleagues feel fully comfortable sharing their challenges and victories. The words and actions of leaders send messages with implications for making colleagues comfortable. Messages are also sent via the structures and processes within the organization that can create disadvantages and reduce inclusivity, or do the opposite.

Examining Structures

Leaders should understand how structural and process elements of their workplace might send non-inclusive messages, or even prevent LGBTQ+ employees from full participation in the organization. Lorenta Soto described how handbooks, training sessions, and organizational artifacts can be examined. Examples include workplace forms only providing male and female checkboxes and name badges that don't allow for go-by names not matching what's on a government ID. Lorena said:

> To create a safe space it has to be in their handbooks that they're not going to tolerate any kind of harassment, bigotry,

or racism. They have to speak specifically to gender identity and sexual orientation. They have to do training about what is acceptable and what is not. It starts with creating a work culture that really is inclusive. Ask people what their pronouns are, what name they prefer on their ID. [Organizations] need to educate themselves.

Lorena also talked about how hiring or advancement processes need to be examined for barriers:

Supervisors need to understand that being queer is going to include baggage. If you want to grow leaders, you need to do certain things. Like people who are going to be promoted to management positions should not be required to have a degree. Right there you're limiting people's ability to grow; often queer people don't have that option, or didn't take it because they got kicked out of their house when their parents found out they were gay. Their family stopped supporting them. They were too afraid to go to college. Criminal background checks also keep people from moving up. Queer people get arrested for being queer. If people tell you that doesn't happen, they're lying to you. It happens. You can move that roadblock out of the way.

Many of these processes or rules are organizational standard practices and leaders may be unaware of their adverse impacts. Fiona Dawson examined a rule in place at the bank she worked for. In this case the bureaucratic requirements made removal of the barrier exceptionally slow, but there was a clear advantage to be gained by the organization if completed.

After coming out to my new boss at a bank in Houston, and having my news received enthusiastically, I turned to my computer to show them an article written about my recent nomination as the 2009 Female Grand Marshal of the Houston LGBT Pride Parade. To my shock and horror the magazine's website was blocked because the bank's servers had labeled any word or acronym related to LGBT as "sexually inappropriate content." I cried a little and requested I get to lead fixing this issue.

A few months later I'm at the bank's headquarters in Birmingham, Alabama having a meeting with the person whose job it is to decide what search words are blocked on the company's network. I wasn't accusatory or aggressive, I simply used my story to help illustrate an example of an LGBTQ person. I gave a short presentation on the biology of gender and sexuality. I was told several bureaucratic steps had to be taken before the engineer had the permission to remove the block, but they would certainly add it to the list of things to do. Many months after, I resigned from my position at the bank because change wasn't happening quickly enough for me.

In reflecting on the organizational barriers he's faced, Russ Houser considered how much potential could be unlocked if those obstacles were removed:

> What would happen if there weren't boundaries in the way? If there were not obstacles preventing people from being themselves and getting done what they needed to do? There'd be so much more positivity, and so much more growth and creativity. If I extrapolate from moments in the classroom where I'm myself and have hopefully inspired a few people...what if that could happen more frequently? It wouldn't be additive or multiplicative, it would be exponential. Those impacts would cascade.

Leaders who remove barriers for their LGBTQ+ colleagues can

provide the catalyst for exponential impacts. Take away obstacles and open the door for the cascade of LGBTQ+ superpowers to come through.

Leaders should examine organizational processes and ask questions. Who developed these processes? Who were these processes implemented to serve? Were the requirements and considerations at the time different than they are now? Who is being disadvantaged by these processes? Jeannie Gainsburg offers what she calls duct-tape patch-up jobs and big fixes for updating policies and processes. She encourages organizations and individuals to examine forms and paperwork, policies, and facilities in relation to LGBTQ+ inclusion. Gainsburg sees it as allies' responsibility to do this work. She wrote:

> I view noninclusive forms as a perfect opportunity to step in with savvy ally action! Why should we leave this educational opportunity to the folks who likely are already feeling extremely stressed and vulnerable? As a straight cisgender ally, I am at extremely low risk for any negative consequences if I advocate for more inclusive forms, so I am the perfect person to do it.[7]

She also includes internal organizational education and promotion of LGBTQ+ imagery as areas to examine. Leaders should take action to patch up issues with duct tape immediately on discovery, and then begin the planning to make big fixes that can unleash the potential of all members of the organization.

Again, if you don't know who might be being disadvantaged, ask. Leaders can enlist the help of LGBTQ+ colleagues or allies in the organization to illuminate these issues. Seek out anyone in the organization who may have deeper awareness and understanding of the relevant concerns and ask them to help.

CHAPTER 13

LGBTQ+ Leadership
in Practice

If there's one thing our contributors' stories make clear, it's that these leaders are always striving to be their best selves. They didn't let societal expectations keep them in boxes that limited their potential. Along the way, they developed leadership superpowers, many of which came from dark places, yet they harnessed them for good. They use these powers for the betterment of people and institutions around them, not selfishly for personal gain. Ultimately, they are people anyone can aspire to be. Today's LGBTQ+ leaders are blazing inspirational trails for future leaders to follow and are driving culture change in ways that benefit all of us.

In this chapter we provide more examples of how developmental journeys produce the leaders our world needs and offer you the opportunity to think about your own development. We provide takeaways specific to LGBTQ+ leaders, but also help allies better understand what LGBTQ+ leaders around them are thinking and experiencing.

LGBTQ+ journeys aren't easy; it's valuable to understand that it can be a grind, not just a few crucible moments. Amanda Fisher puts it into context:

I am lucky to be in a very supportive office with good peers, great supervisors, and hardworking juniors. We have a culture keeping people with biased thoughts from opening their mouths about it. However, systemically, the stress of being threatened with discharge in the wake of the second ban on transgender service after I came out, the difficulty in accessing healthcare, and in general being hassled about a thousand little things related to transitioning, wears me down. As a white person, who tried my best to be sensitive to concepts like systemic racism, they remained just that, conceptual, theoretical. It wasn't until experiencing that visceral sense of deceleration, of friction, around so many things I tried to do, and how over time that wore on my sense of confidence and self-esteem, that I began to understand what systemic oppression really is about. It's not about universally horrific acts like burning crosses and murders, though those certainly happen, but rather the continuous, grinding sense of being hassled, having your basic needs and goals such as a job, healthcare, or promotion be threatened while others around you breeze by with those things simply taken as an expected given. In totality, it's been humbling.

People of color and other marginalized communities face similar hurdles in their developmental journeys and each has unique complexities. With the addition of intersectional identities, developmental journeys become even more distinct from one person to the next. We've all got something to learn from one another and many lessons will resonate across identity groups. One of the best definitions of the leadership development journey comes from an article about learning from leaders of color. Isom, Daniels, and Savage write:

leaders are not solely a product of internal drive; they are also a result of lived experiences, external investment, and recognition. In other words, leaders are made, not born. A person becomes an effective leader through the people that support them and the opportunities and experiences—both good and bad—of their life and career.[1]

We all face myriad influences and must find ways to avoid pitfalls and seize opportunities on the journey.

Playing *Pitfall*

In 1982, *Pitfall* was released on the Atari 2600 gaming system. A handful of blocky pixels named Harry raced through the jungle to collect treasures while constantly jumping over rolling logs or swinging over scorpions lurking in treacherous pits thanks to a helpful rope. Sometimes there was safety underground, but going down there to avoid obstacles might cost the player time they didn't have if they wanted to reach all the treasures. It's a surprisingly apt metaphor for the LGBTQ+ journey: choosing what to avoid, what to hurdle, and when to grab that helpful hand (or rope) to propel you on your journey. Most LGBTQ+ leaders are defined by those choices; not about who they are, but who they reveal themselves to be. Some people are outed by others, maliciously or accidentally, but everyone has choices in how they handle identity management. Descend to safety to avoid potential harm or take a leap of faith that treasures await? "Recognizing coming out and closeting as a continuum reveals some of the ever-present choices inherent to LGBTQ+ lives," wrote Dominic Longo. "LGBTQ+ people continually face the choice of whether to allow themselves to be seen and known as LGBTQ+."[2] If there's a lesson to be learned, it's this: concealment of identity may be necessary at times for safety, but the toll over time can be brutal.

Lord John Browne, former CEO of BP, resigned in 2007 under suspicion of personal and financial misconduct because he couldn't reconcile his public presence with his identity. Interviewed over a decade later, he said:

As I became more well known, I went deep into a hidden, gay life. I then made a whole series of spectacularly bad judgments as a result of that. That is typical of someone who has set to the side a very important part of their life: their identity. It works out very badly.[3]

Following his resignation, Browne set out to rebuild himself and to help create conditions to prevent others from going through what he experienced. In the prologue to *The Glass Closet: Why Coming Out Is Good Business*, Browne said, "I wish I had been brave enough to come out earlier during my tenure... I regret it to this day. I know that if I had done so, I would have made more of an impact for other gay men and women."[4]

Before moving to the private sector, Dayna Walker served in the Army while hiding her transgender and intersex identity. Like Browne, the cost was high:

My shields were up the majority of my career. I was afraid someone might see through the facade. That led to decision-making and day-to-day interactions based on expectations of action rather than potential outcomes. I made poor decisions because of my personal fear and inability to concede what may be construed as weakness.

Fear prevents people from reaching for their best selves. While settling for what's perceived to be acceptable and safe in the moment, regrets and suboptimal decisions become a major drag on lifetime potential and self regard. As with Browne and Dayna hiding their identities, and expressed by Dominic's description of closeting on a continuum, some LGBTQ+ people retreat into the closet even after coming out for their own safety or comfort. Often resulting from external pressures, perceived or real, or the seeking of affirmation of identity from external sources, the retreat can be devastating to the individual. They are now forced to dedicate even more of themselves to suppressing who they are and must focus on appeasing or appealing to others for validation.

An easy area for aspiring LGBTQ+ leaders to fall into this trap is social media. Hatred is far too easy from behind a keyboard and if an individual hasn't developed a strong sense of self-worth or supportive community, the vitriol directed at the LGBTQ+ community can be soul-crushing. Blake Dremann of its power and danger:

> I've come to terms with the fact that while social media does great for change, it's fake. The people who are going to send me nasty things will never interact with me in public. They'll never see me or talk to me. I've told myself to never read the comments because most of those people are mean, horrible people and also 80 percent of them are fake. And the other 20 percent probably don't have the guts to tell you that in person.

LGBTQ+ leaders must build the discipline and internal validation to stand on their own. This is the transformative step of moving beyond the socialized mind that enables them to see the world differently and reach for new opportunities.

Embracing possibilities, racing for treasures in a limited time, supercharges LGBTQ+ leadership development. When captured, the rewards those treasures offer up are impressive. Development of individual superpowers and leadership capacities were explored in Part II; now their true power comes to bear in aggregate.

After Brooklyn Marquis embraced her identity, she said:

> All these hurdles I had to overcome made me stronger and more confident. I gained a lot of respect along the way too from my team. It gave me all these extra tools I almost didn't know I had. It brought the best out in me and gave me so much joy and happiness. It completely transitioned my life from a gender perspective, but it also transitioned my life in confidence, perspective, authenticity, happiness. All of that resonated into exponential growth and success.

There are parallels for all minorities on leadership development journeys. Their superpowers can also come from an understanding of self and embracing identity. Morehouse College president David Thomas said:

> If I have to leave out the part of myself that is positively identified with being Black, then no matter how good I am, I am not the best I can be. I know the power of bringing all of myself, and it becomes a tool that, quite frankly, advantages me over a white guy who has never had to think about his identity.[5]

Alexandria Holder grew into leadership roles after transitioning. She currently supervises junior linguists and says it challenges her every day to draw on her empathy and the management toolkit she's built. But that's not enough. She said, "without the openness I can now express I couldn't effectively do my job." She put a lot of leadership tools in her kit before transitioning, but it was the openness and connection she experienced afterwards that allowed her to utilize them effectively.

Lindsey Medina knew she was gay at the age of eight, but didn't come out until she was 19. It took her 11 years to unapologetically feel comfortable as herself. In high school she struggled because she was always asking herself, "How do I come across as authentic and genuine and get to know people and connect to people without a part of me I'd like to share?" After coming out, Lindsay still faced adversity and lack of acceptance, but persevered. Now an Air Force captain in her mid-twenties, Lindsey reflects on what got her to her current place and how it could have been different. What if there were no pits to fall in, no adversity related to identity? Lindsey believes, in a perfect world, everybody would feel comfortable right off the bat and it wouldn't take as much effort to do what she's done. "[Leadership development] would be more readily available because there isn't discrimination or the perception of other people not accepting you. You can start right off with confidence declaring who you are and what you bring to the table."

Asked if there would be something missing from people who don't go through adversity related to their identity, Michelle Macander was struck by the question. She reframed it:

> Will they not get their superpowers because they didn't face the same adversity? I don't know. Part of what I want to do with my story is ensure people don't need to go through the same things I did. I want them to be coming in as [new leaders] out and proud or in those positions closed to me because I was a gay and female growing up. In the long run it's still a net positive what we're doing, making it easier for them. Hopefully they have less vitriol they have to endure throughout their careers. Some of that makes you a better, more compassionate leader, but some of it will wear on you after a while. So, overall it will be a net positive.

Society is a long way from reaching a point where LGBTQ+ people don't face discrimination and stigmatization. Even then, LGBTQ+ individuals will still have to develop a powerful sense of self through introspection and reflection. That step alone is a huge part of the developmental journey. Our world will never be devoid of adversity and challenges that culminate in personal growth. Everyone faces financial, educational, or personal adversity at one time or another, which they can shrink from or can learn and grow. Author Steve Gavatorta says success arises out of facing and overcoming adversity with grit, hard work, strong will, and persistence. He writes, "adversity, failure, change, and conflict can paradoxically be catalysts for positive things and help us evolve into who we were born to be."[6] So we will never argue for an adversity-free life, but leaders of all varieties should minimize the harms that can occur for LGBTQ+ individuals and ensure the opportunities for growth are clear.

Tempered for Toughness

A powerful way to help people see paths to growth and development is to show them how others made it through those crucibles and emerged tougher. According to the Iowa State Center for Nondestructive Evaluation, toughness is the "ability of a material to absorb energy and deform plastically before fracturing."[7] In other words, it's the ability to bend without breaking. The process to make materials like steel tougher is called tempering. After steel is forged it is heated to a high temperature, but not all the way to its critical (melting) point. This tempering process enhances its ability to withstand stress without catastrophic failure. People can be similarly tempered for toughness through crucible experiences.

Extending the materials science analogy even further, something even better for leaders is to exhibit the resiliency of a viscoelastic material. Viscoelasticity combines the ability to deform under stress and the ability to return to an undeformed state once the stressor is removed. Think of a balloon; when you blow into it and increase the pressure the material expands to handle the pressure, but when the pressure is released gradually the balloon returns back to its original state. Of course, we need to avoid such high loads that the balloon bursts in a catastrophic release of pressure. Harmony is what leaders strive for. That's where the tempering process comes into play and where the power of story to highlight others who have withstood these pressures can make a difference.

Scottie Madden celebrated everyone who lives proudly out:

> We're inspiring every day already. If you come out, especially in this climate, you're going to be basically shooting over your shoulder for the rest of your life. You're constantly justifying your existence. You're constantly justifying why you have a right to live. And we're trying to do this all with children looking at us. So that's why it's up to us to be fierce and proud and out and loud. It fuels the passion. It's why I do this, because you get to see these incredible people doing these incredible things. And even the things that look frivolous like *RuPaul's Drag Race*. There's no frivolity going on there really. That fierceness to live out loud is not about shoes. It's about being all you can be.

Russ Houser explained why telling his own story is so important to support others:

> To be myself was to be out there pushing that envelope daily. It took honest discussions and not being afraid of any topic that students could ask, meeting everything head on and truthfully. That vulnerability, sharing about myself, paid off. There were

always one or two students per class who, even if they weren't out, were happy, or delighted, or relieved that somebody could be out in front of them and be that role model. Those silent students, those are the ones that mattered to me to be open for.

It Gets Better Project is a wonderful example of this process in practice. It Gets Better "envisions a world where all LGBTQ+ youth are free to live equally and know their worthiness and power as individuals."[8] They primarily accomplish their mission through storytelling from LGBTQ+ people who made it through difficulty in their life and found success. It spreads a message: better times are ahead, don't despair. Their work helps build the toughness young LGBTQ+ folks need to persevere and grow into their best future self. Connecting to a better future is most valuable when people are at their most vulnerable, as people in the midst of coming out or transitioning may be.

Kristian Johnsen shares the importance of LGBTQ+ people seeking support amidst those crucible experiences in life.

I know it's a cliché to say it gets better, but it does. You have to go out there and find your family. We all have a blood family, but we all need to find family, those people who understand us and who choose to accept us for who we are. There's people out there for everybody. It's a matter of finding your clique, finding your niche.

We're all going to face struggles. It's keeping things in perspective. As we get older and we have more experiences, it gives us different perspectives. We understand we're all going to face difficult times and there's always going to be something on the other side.

LGBTQ+ LEADERSHIP IN PRACTICE

We're going to have highs; we're going to have lows. It's the lows that make us appreciate the highs more. It's hanging on and finding that support to help you get out of that low, to help pull you up to that next high.

To people who are struggling, whether it's with coming out, family acceptance, mental health issues, food security, or homelessness, whatever people are struggling with, reach out and find the right support networks, find the right people that can help you. Pretty much everything is out there. There's somebody out there to help you get through whatever you're facing.

While we've sought to explain how and why LGBTQ+ leaders develop, the stories are also of people who experienced adversity, found themselves tempered by it, and emerged tougher and more capable on the other side. Their toughness might be exactly what someone needs to hear to understand they too can get through their challenges. Keep in mind, in this context toughness is not the opposite of vulnerability. It simply implies the ability to withstand strain without breaking. We never want to see emerging LGBTQ+ leaders break.

In addition to sharing stories, leaders can metaphorically raise the temperature in their environment to temper their people. They can put people in pressure-filled situations, but with the appropriate support and encouragement needed to grow them without breaking them. Bridgewater CEO Ray Dalio emphasizes development by instilling frank and direct conversations about people's weaknesses as a management practice. While this can be uncomfortable and often takes new employees aback, Dalio says, "most people are happiest when they are improving and doing the things that suit them naturally and help them advance. So learning about your people's weaknesses is just as valuable [for them and for you] as is learning their strengths."9 Leaders who support their people can give projects that stretch individuals skills and capacities without accepting "I don't know how" or "I've never done this before" as an excuse; that's what the support is for.

The tempering heat was high in Brooklyn Marquis' journey, but it didn't melt her. She credits the process for getting her to where she is now:

> It helped me realize even terrifying things can have amazing results. It also gave me a sense of belonging that empowered me with the confidence I needed to get out there and drive more business and revenue than ever. This experience also instilled faith that most people are accepting, open minded, and care enough about others to recognize that happiness is outrageously hard to achieve, and achievement can be vibrant and powerful. Coming out helped me realize I could do anything positive I put my mind to, and it helped me understand you can't ever assume anything about people's heart. It gave me confidence I could hire, lead, and earn the respect of future employees.

Brooklyn's story, and her remarkable success, illustrate the possibilities arising from growing through adversity.

The Heroes We Need

In the world of the X-Men, storied mutant superheroes, Magneto is one of the primary villains. Magneto's backstory is complex; persecuted for being Jewish in Nazi Germany, he was a holocaust survivor and then became the victim of stigmatization and physical abuse for being a mutant. His wounds turned him into "a truly terrifying villain—yet one you completely understand, and even sympathize with."[10] He believes his actions to create a world safe for mutants, no matter how much pain and suffering result, are justified. Fictional villains with similar origin stories abound in pop culture: the Joker, Darth Vader, Hannibal Lecter, and the Grinch, who took away joy after years of it being denied to him. Many of history's greatest monsters could claim the same.

One frequently encountered trauma is hazing, defined as "any activity expected of someone joining or participating in a group that humiliates, degrades, abuses, or endangers them regardless of a person's willingness to participate."[11] A University of Maine study found over half of students involved in clubs, teams, and organizations experienced hazing.[12] So why is hazing so perpetuated and pervasive? Some students said they felt more like part of the group following their hazing. Further, the opportunity for group members to later inflict hazing on others contributes to perpetuation of the cycle. They might even think of hazing as harmless fun. But there is real harm. Another researcher found there has been at least one college hazing death in America every year from 1959 to 2019.[13] That number is likely a small fraction of other harms, like those who didn't make it through the hazing to become part of the club or were deliberately pushed beyond their breaking point. Hazing can be perceived as the price of entry where people feel better about themselves for making it through. They then use that feeling to justify putting others through such onerous practices and the cycle repeats.

How do LGBTQ+ journeys, fraught with perils that could turn them into villains bent on vengeance or passing the pain to the next generation, result instead in a plethora of heroes? LGBTQ+ individuals face humiliation, degradation, abuse, or endangerment, but with no follow-on "reward" to turn straight or cisgender and join the in-group. Survival follows, not reward. Even if they grow from the pain, they probably wish the experiences had never occurred. Somehow, instead of apathy or perpetuating cycles where others face the same level of adversity and pain, they break the cycle. "I don't want anyone else to go through this as a function of something as 'simple' as being gay," said Russ Houser. "I want them to have better challenges. Challenges that inspire them to grow to bigger heights." Everyone faces situations where they're let down by someone who wasn't the ally they were believed to be. LGBTQ+ individuals experience this frequently when rejected by friends or family or when discriminated against for who they are. Yet, instead of framing their negative experiences as something others need to go through, they work to minimize suffering. "I believe everyone should have a standard of living that allows them to feel safe in life," said Melissa Gumbs. "Kids having a space where they can share their concerns or talk about anything safely. That mattered a lot to me and that stemmed from my experience in high school. Not every teacher makes you feel safe. I wanted to find ways to provide those environments."

Lorena Soto is passionate about making sure people in El Paso don't experience the discrimination from individuals and institutions she and others suffered through. In addition to working with the county to hold them accountable to their promises and to enforce the Fair Housing Act, she extends her advocacy to the workplace. She said:

I want to make sure when a company comes to move into this city, that they are going to respect queer rights, that it is in their handbook. That nobody is going to be discriminated against. If they have a history of not doing that, then they can't set up shop here.

Kristian Johnsen feels inherently connected to people who went through significant adversity:

> They went through some crap at some point and they came out the other side a better person, whether it's their identity, being a single mother, or going through mental health struggles. It's all different kinds of things people could potentially go through and become a better person from it. For LGBTQ leaders, that's something I know inherently they've gone through. Even if we have the most accepting family, even if we've never faced overt discrimination, there's just day-to-day challenges we face as members of the LGBTQ community.

Kristian uses his experiences to challenge the way things have always been done and to figure out how to overcome inherent barriers so others don't face the same challenges.

Leadership, and the abilities and capacities necessary to lead, are not inherently good or evil. People look to ethics and motivation, the intent behind the leadership, as a determinant of the moral quality. When leadership focuses on the betterment of others, just about any moral standard says that's the right kind of leadership.

The developmental experiences of LGBTQ+ leaders push their focus outward and away from the self. They prioritize team success, not themselves. Without this focus, it would be easy to use the skills they learned for nefarious or selfish purposes. For example, the hypersensitivity to the environment many LGBTQ+ leaders have is typically used to understand an audience or to connect on an individual level by picking up on subtle clues. However, this skill set could easily be used to manipulate people into taking actions not in their best interest. Recall the story where a slight rise in color in a person's face and neck signaled a reason to dive a little deeper to figure out what was going on. That same ability could help realize when someone has struck a nerve that could be exploited to get what they want. Many other skills developed through the crucibles faced by LGBTQ+ leaders could also be used to pursue selfish goals. Yet these are not their choices.

Becky Burke frames her choice to support others as a gift. "I've been given this gift to impact other people. Having the ability and not doing it would just be a waste of some positive energy we could put into this world. I think we need a lot more of it." The examples described in this book are bountiful evidence that LGBTQ+ leaders like Becky are the heroes people crave.

Perhaps more than anything, what makes them the leaders people want is that they don't lead in a way that makes others follow, but in a way that enables others to go beyond. A person can get people to follow them, at least for a while, through rewards, threats, or sheer charisma. But that's not the leader you want. Kathi Lake, a transgender woman and environmental engineer, said:

I was never someone people would naturally follow. I wasn't charismatic or funny or good looking. Even after emulating the various types of people—the joker, the party-goer, the strict and by-the-book taskmaster—I found the greatest success in being myself: the dedicated worker with a nurturing streak. People followed me because they knew I could fix the problem and I made sure their needs were taken care of. To be honest, they also enjoyed my chocolate chip cookies. Sure, you can lead through fear and coercion—believe me, I've seen it, but that's a short-term strategy. The leader with their people's interests at heart will have a team willing to follow them through any trial.

Jonathan Droomgoole believes LGBTQ+ leaders stand out for the right reasons. He wrote, "We want to take up space and cause good trouble, uplift, and bring our community along, and not forget that we stand on the shoulders of the generations of leaders that came before."[14]

LGBTQ+ leaders forge bonds with people and create teams willing to go through the toughest challenges to succeed together. Through trying times, they build and develop people to take the team further than they ever could. Good leaders build their replacement, great leaders pave paths, making it easier for their successor to go beyond where they ever reached. Growing up, Lindsey Medina rarely saw leaders who looked like her, or got to know people who had experienced similar challenges:

> I was often finding my own way through the difficulties of sexism, racism, and coming out in a primarily white and Christian community. I developed a thick skin, and learned how to work with people I disagreed with. Often I was the first girl, LGTBQ+ member, or Latina to accomplish whatever I did. I hated being the first. But I made sure to let others know how I did it, to keep the door open for more to follow.

Lindsey was passing on what she learned and kicking down barriers so others didn't have to face the hurdles that slowed her down or sapped her energy.

Elisa Hebert, a queer woman and vice president of engineering operations at a technology firm, offers advice to queer leaders about the most powerful thing they can do. She exhorts them, "Use the space you found for yourself to create new space for others. Always put your hand out. You stood on the shoulders of giants, now be that giant for others." Leaders like Elisa who extend their hand, pull others up, and encourage them onwards are the heroes we need.

CHAPTER 14

Champions of the Long Game

In a 2016 keynote speech at the United Conference on Aids, Melissa Harris-Perry said:

> Here is the good news. The struggle continues. Nobody promised you would get to live during the part of the revolution when we were winning. You are promised that people worked hard before you. Your responsibility is that during your part you take the baton. You do not have to do it alone.[1]

Taking the baton implies that the work is a relay race. We have to build upon the work of the people who came before us and trust the people who come after us to carry on after our time is past.

Part III offered practical guidance to capitalize upon and extend the positive impacts of LGBTQ+ leaders. It highlighted how to remove obstacles, draw value from diverse experiences and perspectives, and empower LGBTQ+ colleagues. Our contributors graciously shared their stories, and we are privileged to pay it forward by sharing our contributors' recommendations and requests about what allies, advocates, and leaders can do to continue this work. Together, we play the long game to advance opportunity and dignity for all of us. Jonathan Dromgoole, author of Out to Lead, put it this way: "Those of us who have the privilege to live as our authentic selves also have the responsibility to lead and pave the path for future generations and make welcoming spaces for others to come out."[2]

When writing we were stumped about what word best represented allies, advocates, and leaders because saying that over and over is a mouthful. So we asked our newly released AI overlords. Surprisingly, they all agreed! ChatGPT, Google's Bard, and Microsoft's Bing chatbots, all said "champions." According to ChatGPT:

> Champions are individuals or groups who actively support and promote a cause or idea, often using their influence and leadership skills to bring attention to important issues and drive positive change. They can be allies by standing with and supporting marginalized communities, leaders by taking charge and mobilizing others towards a common goal, and advocates by speaking out and raising awareness on important issues."[3]

Brilliant! So, what can we all do to be champions?

Maintaining Energy

The work of LGBTQ+ leaders and champions involves near-constant energy expenditure. Continual cultural or political backlash and steps backward can be truly draining, but it's important to understand these as inherent parts of the process. Therefore, self-care and deliberate ways of thinking about ways to recharge are critical. Matthew Rose said:

> Every social movement faces a backlash after significant victories. If you didn't have backlash then what was really holding you back in the beginning? So, we have to keep pushing on

that. And recognize it is worth the fight. It is worth the energy. It is worth the effort.

Tamara Adrian took this a step further, acknowledging backlashes, but emphasizing, "If you do not act, things will never improve. They can even get worse."

Raffi Freedman-Gurspan spoke about the importance of stepping back:

We rotate people off the front lines for a reason. We all hit moments where we need to take care of ourselves and some of us are scared to admit that. We don't necessarily want to show weakness. But as I said to a colleague many years ago, "You're of no service to us if you burn out." I believe that people should be good to themselves, because that's what we're fighting for at the end of the day—goodness for all of us, and being good to each other. One cannot do that if one is not good to themselves.

Similarly, Paula M. Neira explained how her position in the fight has shifted over time; she now sees her role as encouraging others and helping them develop realistic perspectives. Paula specifically encouraged taking utilitarian and pragmatic perspectives about the ongoing fight:

We need to set realistic expectations... One of the toughest things to learn, for those who have been the victim of injustice—justice is never going to come fast enough. And for some people justice is never going to come in their lifetime. That's a horrible, horrible lesson to learn. It's one of the cruel lessons you have to learn if you're going to be a leader in a social justice space. But that doesn't mean you give up. It means I'm going to fight the battle today and I'm going to try to win what I can win today.

This theme recurred in several conversations and emphasized the importance of taking a long view.

Dominic Longo offered perspective on needing fulfillment and purpose to help maintain energy:

Looking at myself and my peers I noticed so many queer folks languishing. There seems to be a kind of yearning and emptiness not being filled by the life that was offered to them. And too few resources or communities seemed to address that wanting for meaning, for purpose, for connection, for intimacy that any human being has, but that has its own flavor for LG-BTQ folks. So it was the move from languishing to flourishing that I thought was a gap in the support structures in the communities. So that's the place where I started.

Providing this support is a key part of Dominic's work in leader development, as is helping people recharge for the long run and build community.

Building Community

Steven Yacovelli wrote, "Perhaps great LGBTQ+ leadership is really all about relationships. Great LGBTQ+ Leaders are the ones who know their people, cultivate long-term relationships, and then use the connections to help all involved reach the heights of potential."[4] Our contributors repeatedly highlighted relationships as essential to overcoming adversity and helping them move forward.

Tamara Adrian encouraged champions to seek connection:

No person is an island. You have to do this in collaboration with all the persons you need in order to avoid backlashes. In order to impede those forces who are denying your existence... If you see the woods and not the trees, you start to understand at this moment you cannot do it alone. You have to create the widest possible number of alliances and the widest possible number of collaborations in all fields.

Similarly, Melissa Gumbs spoke about allyship as action: "I need you to link arms with me on the front line and charge forward. It's not just me. It has to be all of us."

Building community was Matthew Rose's primary imperative:

First and foremost we are a community. Get yourself a tight circle that you can talk to. You have people who understand what it means to be a leader and to go through it. You need support... Finding people who you can be authentic, honest, and just say the shit to and they'll say the shit back to you. They will tell you... Because it is hard to be a leader; especially, the higher you climb the more challenging it can be. So it's just nice to have people who understand.

Dominic Longo highlighted how cultivating a queer community, which he calls the "Pride Tribe," can sustain you and help you develop and grow:

The thing we can do to help each other is, first of all, see each other. In our yearning, in our wanting, to see the depths of each other. And second, to have thoughtful conversations of care, and vulnerability, and opening, and inquiring. Like, "You just don't seem that joyful these days. What's going on for you, friend?" That kind of reflective deeper conversation I think is one of the greatest gifts that we can exchange with one another... This is part of what we look to community for.

How can champions make sure LGBTQ+ leaders have the support they need, not only from within their community, but all around? Everyone can move the needle forward. As Jeannie Gainsburg describes, anyone can be an ally:

> Typically when we see the word *ally* in the context of LGBTQ+ advocacy, we think only of the person who is straight (i.e., heterosexual) and not transgender. However, we *all* can be LGBTQ+ allies, even if we are a part of the LGBTQ+ communities. If you are a lesbian, you can be an ally to the bisexual/pansexual communities. If you are a white transgender woman, you can support and advocate for transgender women of color.[5]

Champions must encourage everyone to think about the roles they fill as allies and advocates.

Everyone Has a Role

Just as understanding diverse perspectives is key for leaders, diversity of skill set and roles within LGBTQ+ advocacy are key to success. Blake Dremman highlighted how important this is:

> There are certain groups of people you need to push a movement forward. You need loud and proud people to get attention and you need folks who are calm, composed, and practical to sit at the table and talk it out. What are people's concerns? What are their issues? Come to a level of understanding to bring about what needs to happen. It may be slow, but it's generally successful.

Sometimes allies are needed to lead in places LGBTQ+ folks can't go or don't exist. Scottie Jeanette Madden said:

That's really the power of allyship and why it's so critical. Because others will follow our allies more so than they will follow us. It takes our allies to stand up and say, "Actually no, no, that's incorrect." Allies are probably our most important asset, because non-LGBTQIA+ people will listen to them. That's the necessary component.

Champions helping people understand there is a place for them in making change, no matter how they show up, is vital. Ross Murray shared, "Most everyday people get overwhelmed. They're scared of doing it wrong, or they're comparing themselves to someone else who's doing more or better. They see giants in our history like Martin Luther King, Jr. or Gandhi, and they're like 'Well I could never do that.'" It's important to give people a specific role or action, and Ross explains how there are many different ways to engage:

I would much rather do my advocacy behind the scenes— maybe direct the information. We need all those types. Advocacy is not just one thing. It is many, many, many things and I'm trying to give people ideas about one of the many things that they could be doing. That's what goes into the everyday advocate.

It's essential to help people understand they can enter this work with whatever strengths or skills they have available.

Paula M. Neira emphasized capitalizing on unique strengths:

As a leader, allow people to play to their strengths. I would not be very good at going to a grassroots community movement meeting. That ain't my forte. Talking at higher levels, looking at policy and systemic change, as opposed to being down on the grassroots is playing to my strength. There are other people who do that really well, so allow them to learn and use their strengths. Realize that the whole spectrum of contributions is what eventually changes big systems. You need the person who's going to stand outside and yell, and you need the person in the conference room who is having the conversation. The person inside the conference room is going to be impactful in bringing about change, but you need the other folks to keep the spotlight on the conversation, to hold people accountable, and to rally people to the fight.

From marches, to meetings, to national and global policy-making, there are roles to fill and the right people to fill them.

Blake Dremman sees LGBTQ+ leadership roles in advocacy changing over time, especially once progress is made. "For acceptance to be an everyday thing, we're not there yet. We won't be there for probably several decades because we're still battling about whether we even deserve to exist right now. We [still] have a lot of firsts. Let's move beyond the firsts." So, once you can see your ability to fill a role—any role—how can you help move beyond the firsts?

Elevating Voices

For champions, it's important to elevate the voices of marginalized people and bring them to the conversation. Matthew Rose talked about why this is critical, and how to do it:

> Sometimes we need people to acknowledge that we're here. We deserve a space and a voice at the table because we're doing all of the work. And when we have that voice at the table, it brings so much more to the work. It brings perspectives you never even thought about or considered. As people who usually have

to deal with oppression just because we show up, or the fact that we often have to explain things (like terminology or pronouns). It's bringing these things to attention to people in ways that really matter... Even just the approach to which we come by something can be pivotal to actually changing the dialogue and giving us that move forward.

Matthew also explained the need to be deliberate about how we elevate those voices:

> Super important is making space that recognizes people have a lot of identities. You might want to talk about all of them or you might not want to talk about all of them. But the space to do that and the skills to know how to navigate in between all of those are really helpful. We uniquely need to have the space to know when you want to deploy your identity, and how you want to deploy your identity. We should know and have skills and training to teach us how we can bring it up. What are ways we can bring it up that can be seen and heard, but don't also [make you] be the standard bearer for all of it?

He explained how queer folks are often forced into doing extra work, because just showing up can be a political statement in and of itself. He asks us to consider several questions. How do you broaden the work? Who's not at the table? Who needs to be at the table? How do you really push for shared community needs? How do we move the whole table together? This harkens back to Jennifer L. Dane's notion of smashing the current table and building a new one! Rose notes, "It's about never leaving people behind. We have to meet people where they're at because if we don't, we leave them there. It is possible to both uplift and bring people forward."

Indeed, elevating voices is more than involving their essential perspectives in conversations. It's also about helping people to move forward and, as Dominic Longo describes, to flourish:

> Even as more and more young folks today are identifying as queer, [I hope] that need not become a new stricture. That there always be space. That we leave space for the wondrous weirdness of every person to bloom, to flourish, to come forward, to be whatever they might be. There will be, if we let them, kinds of human beings that the world has never seen before. That's happening even now. It is for us to raise up each other and not rely on what we know, on what we have seen before. But to be genuinely, deeply, passionately curious, who are you? Who's in there wanting to come out? Whoever you are. That's the future of queer flourishing that I hope for.

That's the future champions understand is best for all of us and are willing to fight for.

Broadening Our Understanding

Whether already actively engaged in allyship and advocacy or just starting out, champions benefit from broadened understanding of the big ideas that inform the work. A greater appreciation of LGBTQ+ leadership dynamics can improve champions' ability to communicate key concepts. Some LGBTQ+ leaders have "big ideas" we think enhance understanding and better prepare everyone to inspire and tell powerful stories.

These big-picture ideas are some of the most inspiring and impactful messages we share. Paula M. Neira explored the value of messaging ideas effectively:

It's humanity. Just bombarding somebody with facts and figures, that's easy to ignore. When you're able to share the impact of these decisions on real people...you're playing on that
emotional, as well as intellectual level. To raise their awareness
to get them to enlightened self-interest. "Here's why this is
such a good idea for you"—why we need to be more aware,
why we need to be more inclusive, why we need to change
these systems so that more people can benefit. Finding the
argument that resonates with your audience.

Part of expanding our understanding is knowing fact from fiction
and addressing abundant falsehoods. Blake Dremann said:

> Every time someone lends some weird, unfounded accusation
> or prediction of what it's going to be like to allow LGBTQ people
> to exist in public they've been wrong. Every single time. All
> the predictions about what would happen if we allowed gay
> marriage, if we allowed gays in the military, if we allowed trans
> people in the military. Every prediction made by the church
> has been wrong. The world is still moving, the country is still
> here, nothing has happened. They've been wrong and guess
> what, we still allow them to make it. We still give it credence
> and we still allow people to debate us on national television.
> And none of the media, or even our politicians, have called
> it out. [They haven't said] "You have been wrong. It's false.
> It's made up." We aren't doing that forcefully enough and we
> continue to allow them to have a stage where those things are
> viewed as true. And the only way that we are going to win is
> for us to start telling people that they've been wrong.

Raffi Freedman-Gurspan explained the importance of champions
engaging fully in these conversations. "I hope allies don't shy away

from having conversations about all types of difference, not just LGBTQ related. I'd encourage allies to be aware of their place in conversations. While sometimes it's inappropriate to speak on behalf of other people if you don't know their experience, in other ways we absolutely need people standing shoulder to shoulder with us, and even being courageous resistors themselves. Also, ask what you can do as an ally. Just first being present, and then asking, "What can I do?" goes such a long way.

By being present, asking questions, and working to understand these stories, champions are better prepared to show up and get involved. Further, by learning about queer stories champions can connect them with their own. Shared experiences help people tell their own story and show up authentically in the work. Blake Dremann noted the importance of getting deeply involved in local organizations as an ally. He said, "One thing that LGBTQ kids don't ever see is straight allies who come and volunteer with them. Who have no interest other than their ability to help you succeed." Champions are the people who show up and encourage others to do so as well.

Champions think about how they can move others into allyship. Ross Murray encourages champions to learn people's values and motivations. "We really have to understand. You learn what people care about...to know where they are and how to move them forward [toward] allyship. We can't use the same argument for everyone. We need to do a lot more customization." He says champions have to have one-on-one conversations and help people connect the things they care about with this work. Tamara Adrian makes a similar point:

I started by asking myself how to be tolerant with intolerant people. That's a huge challenge for someone who predicates tolerance as a tool for changing the world. Especially when you've faced various forms of intolerance, even people who are ready to kill you if they could. So how to be tolerant with the intolerant? To answer that question I started to understand that those who are *actually* intolerant are surrounded by other people who only mimic their intolerance. Strategically I started to reach those others that could be convinced. You have to understand the needs of the other. Then you are able to enter into a process of negotiation, even with those who are intolerant. You can find ways to create alliances.

Not knowing their role, the discomfort of not having enough knowledge or a strong enough connection to the community, and the fear of getting it wrong can hold individuals back, and keep them from becoming champions. People exist on a spectrum of support for LGBTQ+ rights, from champion to die-hard opponent. When champions are ready, they work alongside LGBTQ+ leaders to change tolerance or near-allyship into full championship, allyship, and inclusion. As Jeannie Gainsburg, a champion, points out: "The more we learn about LGBTQ+ individuals and communities, the better we become at changing hearts and minds outside those communities. We can help bridge the gap between these two worlds and aid in understanding and communication."[6]

This Isn't the End

LGBTQ+ leaders have been around forever. Like the rate of left-handedness in the population, which was beaten away by teachers for generations, it's only when society accepts them and the punishment stops that they appear in their true numbers.[7]

Leaders like our contributors, and the champions they inspire, are setting the stage for future flourishing, just as all the titans of history have done for them. Today's champions are doing their work to bend the long moral arc of the universe, but are nowhere near done.

Matthew Rose reminds us that:

> LGBT folks have existed the entire course of human history. There are drawings. There are writings. We are literally everywhere, but only in the modern century did anyone raise the question of rights for us. The fact that people are just considering our rights means it's gonna be a bumpy road for a while. Because that means that they never considered that your dignity and identity were not being met before. And we're saying we're fed up and we want it. But we're not asking for special rights. We're asking for recognition of the ability to do what everyone else does—get up in the morning. Go get some coffee, maybe pick up some groceries, walk a dog, walk a cat, just go about and exist. Having us show up in more places to remind people that we literally have always been everywhere. We are who we are. We have great ideas to bring. Help remind people of the importance in our shared humanity.

Paula M. Neira explains the long game in this way:

> It's a long, long struggle. We use the terms of war and battle when we're describing this because it really is on some level a struggle [against] regression and ignorance. The military is better, is stronger [since] we've allowed people who were different to actually be themselves and contribute. And the same applies in the civilian world. How do you change systems and structures to allow people to do it? That's the ongoing fight.

She says that in order to change the system you have to offer approaches that are going to actually achieve something for somebody, highlighting that often that means progress in a series of small wins.

Champions can maintain energy by remembering that those small wins are part of something so much larger. Tamara Adrian told us:

> We are not now fighting for LGBTI rights. We are fighting for human rights at large. You take into account many points of view. Not only of course LGBTI people, but all people. People who are coming from very different environments and with very different perspectives. That's the goal of a social movement. Putting people together so they are part of a larger group of groups. They can start to encompass the fight of the other groups and create a common goal.

Matthew Rose also shared that champions can get through it with the right mindset:

> You've got to play the long game and you're in it for the long haul. Your part of the work matters and is a legacy. But you do it in community and together. You're all linked by who came before you and who's gonna come after you. In that long arc of history, you're gonna matter.

Maintain energy, build community, find a role, elevate voices, keep learning, and play the long game. Each of these big ideas is ripe for deeper exploration, rich discussion, or perhaps future research. There are so many LGBTQ+ leadership stories yet to be explored and we hope you will keep exploring them alongside us. The current social climate in the United States and around the world demands it. We're at a time where we've seen the value of

CHAMPIONS OF THE LONG GAME

LGBTQ+ leadership and how it helps everyone flourish. Yet the backlash to that visibility and progress is very real and very scary. Hatred, fear, and ignorance toward the LGBTQ+ community has not disappeared and its forces are fighting the hardest they can right now to roll back the clock.

Existence is resistance, but leadership is needed to ensure that the gains of the past half-century are broadened, deepened, and cemented in place as we build upon them for the future. The LGBTQ+ people around you who have been forged in the fire of adversity will be more than happy to help by using their leadership superpowers. Their stories are powerful and create the impact the world needs to move us all toward greater flourishing. They're geared to pave the path so that others may follow them and go further. In the meantime, champions can take inspiration from these words, courageously step into the unknown future, and get to work.

Epilogue

Be the Goat

Jude Hope Harris

For the last 15 years I worked in Hollywood as a producer and entertainment executive, producing movies, shows, and digital series for MTV, Netflix, Hulu, Starz, Showtime, and Comedy Central. I spent most of those years living as a straight, white male. Three years ago, at age 42, I came to understand myself as transgender and began the process of transitioning while continuing my work. This process has been painful, awkward, embarrassing, funny, and full of moments of extraordinary kindness and grace.

It's sad to say, but it's unlikely I would be where I am in my career if I had been living authentically all these years. Many of the people who were quick to forgive my shortcomings when they perceived me as a cis man were also most able to ignore my successes as a trans woman. None of this is surprising, of course, but I must acknowledge that any advice I offer from my experience as a trans woman comes from someone who has had a uniquely privileged experience as such. I'm encouraged by the many young trans and gender non-conforming interns, producers, and young executives and I'm excited to see the ways they change our industry for the better.

The best advice I can offer on what leadership looked like for me in these last three gloriously queer years doesn't come from a Netflix office or movie set. It comes from my best friend, Lee Hennessy, a goat farmer in rural New York. Lee deserves to be enshrined in American lore alongside Paul Bunyan and Pecos Bill. He is often a one-man operation, who knows his over a hundred goats by name and recognizes the sounds of each of their voices. His days are spent carrying 75-pound buckets of feed and water, seeing the herd safely through kidding season, protecting the animals from the elements and the occasional predator, while day after day making the most delicious cheese you've ever tasted.

Without Lee, I'm not sure where I'd be. I might not be at all. Lee talked me through all the hardest moments of my divorce, the mental health toll accompanying my coming out experience, and the bumpy adjustment from being "one of the guys" to anything but. On one of our many phone calls, he told me, "When I have to get the herd through flood waters, or thunder, or past the scent of a coyote—I just need one goat to walk ahead of the rest and the others will follow. It doesn't have to be the queen goat, the biggest goat, or the bravest goat, just the goat that's ready to put one foot in front of the other and walk through the scary thing." I don't remember which scary thing I was facing when he offered this advice, but he concluded, "Boo, you've got to be the goat."

So, in my darkest days, I tried to be the goat: to realize my job was not to know how every step of the process would work, but to merely pick a direction, put one foot in front of the other, and walk until I'd gotten somewhere better.

"Be the goat" carried me through the strange dance of figuring out how to operate as a trans person without much lived experience of transness. What does one do when a colleague asks about your plans for your genitals? When meetings descend into a pronoun salad full of promises that the offender always gets it right (when you're not around)? When each bruise on your ego scarcely has time to heal before you earn another one. In so many fundamentally uncool situations, "Be the goat" helped me to make things cool. It wasn't immediate. It took practice. There were days when the storms raged too wildly and wolves were too frightening. But day after day, I practiced. And soon, to paraphrase Brené Brown, I was teaching people to give me the dignity I was worthy of receiving. Worthy not because I was beautiful or passable or had transition or my identity remotely figured out. Worthy because I had put one foot in front of the other, and moved through the fear.

Lee's advice to "be the goat" is excellent for any dark day when all you can do is hope for a better future and start walking in that general direction, past sharp teeth and thunderstorms. But being the goat isn't just about the dark days. It's the most helpful advice I received about the unknowns of transition and its life-altering decisions that require imagining an outcome you've never experienced and can hardly imagine.

Lee's brave, dumb, reckless goat isn't walking alone. When she steps into the unknown, her sisters follow. Because generations of evolution have taught these ruminants that falling in step with this wild outlier is actually a good idea. There is food for them on the other side of that unknown, or shelter, or a mate. When one goat follows the goatherd's call, the others follow that goat into something better.

A reasonable question at this point might be "Why not just be the goatherd?" First, and foremost: because that's an objectively less catchy mantra. But we're never the goatherd in the most creative endeavors in our own lives, as individuals or as part of an organization. Whether we set out in search of authenticity or love, the next great screenplay, or the successful launch of a new division—if we're living well we don't know exactly what will happen. We likely have visions of how those things will go, perhaps with large parts of the plan mapped out. Large stretches of the journey might be frictionless, easy to entice others to join. Who doesn't love a brainstorming session? A kickoff meeting? A mandate from on high, dripping with the potential to succeed, grow, flourish? These are all intoxicating moments in any process. My least favorite leaders have all loved to be part of the energy of a new venture. They've been less enthusiastic about the real work of moving through the frightening unknown.

What, today, isn't a frightening unknown? Even the most ordinary work days happen in the midst of social, political, epidemiological, and environmental events that have disrupted any semblance of what generations have perceived as "normal." And for those of us fortunate enough to work in fields adaptable to these changes, we're all carrying some amount of anxiety, even trauma, as we make our way through the work week. That burden, like so many, increases inversely proportional to the privilege of the worker.

Once, in my pre-transition life, I alerted a network head to the ways finance policies were eroding vendor trust and making a certain kind of agile production impossible. I asked him to work with the finance and legal teams to change the policies so I could create the kinds of projects he wanted. His response was "You're bringing me problems. I need you to bring me solutions." His tenure ended in less than a year, but his response stuck with me.

Of course, real leadership isn't about telling subordinates to figure things out on their own. I have worked with many high-level executives who think asking for an outcome is enough. This isn't leadership. At best, it is coaching. I believe that approach to management, more than the longstanding issues of under-compensation, lack of employer loyalty, and decreasing benefits, is driving the "great resignation."

Those of us who have adapted to living atypical lives are uniquely qualified to lead in atypical times. We may not be the queen, the strongest, or the bravest, but we are all working alongside people who want us to take a step into the unknown, and who are eager to follow. Like Lee's goats, we aren't where we want to be. The status quo isn't working for many people and polling suggests most don't think the state of the world is trending positive. The world is hungry for people brave enough to step into the unknown. They are ready to follow. We are already leading.

Further Reading

Badgett, M. V. Lee (2020). *The Economic Case for* LGBT *Equality*. Boston, MA: Beacon Press.

Baldock, Kathy (2014). *Walking the Bridgeless Canyon: Repairing the Breach between the Church and the* LGBT *Community*. Reno, NV: CanyonWalker Press.

Brown, Jennifer (2022). *How to Be an Inclusive Leader*. Oakland, CA: Berrett-Koehler Publishers, Inc.

Dromgoole, Jonathan (2021). *Out to Lead: Shaping Queer Leadership*. Washington, DC: New Degree Press.

Gainsburg, Jeannine (2023). *The Savvy Ally*. Lanham, MD: Rowman & Littlefield.

Gelwicks, Andrew (2020). *The Queer Advantage*. New York: Hachette Book Group.

Tannehill, Brynn (2018). *Everything You Ever Wanted to Know about Trans (But Were Afraid to Ask)*. London: Jessica Kingsley Publishers.

Yacovelli, Steve (2019). *Pride Leadership: Strategies for the* LGBTQ+ *Leader to Be the King or Queen of Their Jungle*. Hartford, CT: Publish Your Purpose Press.

Endnotes

Preface

1. www.forgedinfire.org/podcast.html

Chapter 1

1. Trump, D. [@RealDonaldTrump] (2017, July 26). After consultation with my Generals and military experts, please be advised that the United States Government will not accept or allow... [Tweet]. https://twitter.com/realDonaldTrump/status/890193981585444864
2. Fram, B., & Embser-Herbert, M. (2020). *With Honor and Integrity: Transgender Troops in Their Own Words* (pp. 149–150). New York University Press.
3. Benjamin, S. (2007, June 8). Don't ask, don't translate. *New York Times*. www.nytimes.com/2007/06/08/opinion/08benjamin.html
4. Rost, J. C. (1991). *Leadership for the Twenty-First Century* (1st edn.) (p. 104). Praeger.
5. US Army (2019, May 7). Q. Who First Originated the Term VUCA (Volatility, Uncertainty, Complexity and Ambiguity)? US Army War College. https://usawc.libanswers.com/faq/84869
6. Congressional Future of Defense Task Force (2019, October 21). The Future of Defense Task Force—Discussion. *Washington Daybook*. www.proquest.com/docview/2307157842
7. Gelwicks, A. (2020). *The Queer Advantage* (p. 176). Hachette Book Group.

Chapter 2

1. NASA (n.d.). STS-7 Mission Archive. www.nasa.gov/mission_pages/shuttle/shuttlemissions/archives/sts-7.html
2. University of California Television. (2017, September 1). Honoring Sally:

Tam O'Shaughnessy aboard the R/V Sally Ride [Video file]. YouTube. www.youtube.com/watch?v=oZ7PWRZHEnA

3. UC San Diego (n.d.). 20th Anniversary: Sally Ride Science @ UC San Diego. Sally Ride Science. https://sallyridescience.ucsd.edu/20th-anniversary

4. O'Shaughnessey, T. (2021, June 24). Loving Sally Ride. NPR. www.npr.org/2021/06/22/1009098412/loving-sally-ride

5. ibid.

6. University of California Television (2017, September 1). Honoring Sally: Tam O'Shaughnessy aboard the R/V Sally Ride [Video file]. YouTube. www.youtube.com/watch?v=oZ7PWRZHEnA

7. O'Shaughnessey, T. (2021, June 24). Loving Sally Ride. NPR. www.npr.org/2021/06/22/1009098412/loving-sally-ride

8. Gates, G. (2011, April 1). How many people are lesbian, gay, bisexual, and transgender? Williams Institute. https://williamsinstitute.law.ucla.edu/wp-content/uploads/How-Many-People-LGBT-Apr-2011.pdf

9. Anderson, L., File, T., Marshall, J., McElrath, K., & Scherer, Z. (2021, November 4). New Household Pulse Survey data reveals differences between LGBT and non-LGBT respondents during COVID-19 pandemic. United States Census Bureau. www.census.gov/library/stories/2021/11/census-bureau-survey-explores-sexual-orientation-and-gender-identity.html

10. Human Rights Campaign Foundation (2021, December 8). *We Are Here: Understanding The Size Of The LGBTQ+ Community*. HRC. https://hrc-prod-requests.s3-us-west-2.amazonaws.com/We-Are-Here-120821.pdf

11. Cantarella, E. (1992). *Bisexuality in the Ancient World* (p. 211). Yale University Press.

12. Wohl, V. (2002). *Love among the Ruins: The Erotics of Democracy in Classical Athens* (p. 6). Princeton University Press.

13. Greenberg, D. F. (2008). *The Construction of Homosexuality* (p. 129). University of Chicago Press.

14. Museum of London (2020). *What Does Emperor Hadrian's Preference for Male Same-Sex Relationships Reveal about the Attitudes of Roman Londoners?* www.museumoflondon.org.uk/application/files/1516/0380/9715/lr-secondary-schools-teacher-resources-lgbt-history-hadrian.pdf

15. Cantarella, E. (1992). *Bisexuality in the Ancient World* (p. 177). Yale University Press.

16. ibid.

17. Fone, B. (2000). *Homophobia: A History* (p. 11). Metropolitan Books.

18. ibid. (239).

19. ibid. (411).

20. Washington, G. "George Washington to Baron Steuben, 23 December 1783," *The Writings of George Washington from the Original Manuscripts*, Vol. 27, ed.

John C. Fitzpatrick (p. 283) (Washington, DC: Government Printing Office, 1931–1944).

21. Breneman, W. (2012). *Male-Male Intimacy in Early America* (p. 107). Routledge.

22. Morgan, T. (2018, June 1). Why MLK's right-hand man, Bayard Rustin, was nearly written out of history. Sky History. www.history.com/news/bayard-rustin-march-on-washington-openly-gay-mlk

23. Rustin, B. (1986, February 7). Black history in the making. *Washington Blade*, 1. https://digdc.dclibrary.org/islandora/object/dcplisland ora%3A10542?#page/1/mode/1up

24. ibid.

25. Hendrix, S. (2011, August 21). Bayard Rustin, organizer of the March on Washington, was crucial to the movement. *Washington Post*. www.washing tonpost.com/lifestyle/style/bayard-rustin-organizer-of-the-march-on-wash ington-was-crucial-to-the-movement/2011/08/17/glQAooZ7UJ_story.html

26. Office of the Federal Register (2011, August 21). Executive Order 10450— Security Requirements for Government Employment. National Archives. www.archives.gov/federal-register/codification/executive-order/10450.html

27. Osburn, C. D. (2021). *Mission Possible* (p. 140). C. Dixon Osburn.

28. US Supreme Court (2022, June 24). Dobbs, State Health Officer of the Mississippi Department of Health, et al. v. Jackson Women's Health Organization et al. Supremecourt.gov. www.supremecourt.gov/opinions/21pdf/19-1392_6j37.pdf

Chapter 3

1. Crucible (2023). In Merriam-Webster.com. www.merriam-webster.com/dictionary/crucible

2. Hendel-Giller, R. (2017, August). Vertical Development for Leaders. Actionable. https://conversations.actionable.co/thoughts/2017/08/vertical-development-leaders

3. Kegan, R. (1994). *In Over Our Heads: The Mental Demands of Modern Life*. Harvard University Press.

4. ibid.

5. Hendel-Giller, R. (2017, August). Vertical Development for Leaders. Actionable. https://conversations.actionable.co/thoughts/2017/08/vertical-development-leaders

6. Cavallaro, L. and French, B. (2021). The impact of graduate education on the mental complexity of mid-career military officers. *Journal of Adult Development*. https://rdcu.be/ciSVu

7. Kegan, R. (1994). *In Over Our Heads: The Mental Demands of Modern Life*. Harvard University Press.

8. Anderson, D., & Ackerman Anderson, L. (2013). Leadership Breakthrough: Meeting the Transformational Challenges of the 21st Century Security Environment. In Wells, L., Hailes, T. C., & Davies, M. C. (eds.) *Changing Mindsets to Transform Security: Leader Development for an Unpredictable and Complex World*, pp. 25–52 (p. 41). National Defense University. https://ndupress. ndu.edu/Portals/68/Documents/Books/CTBSP-Exports/Changing-Mind sets-to-Transform-Security.pdf?ver=2017-06-16-104715-250

9. Hendel-Giller, R. (2017, August). Vertical Development for Leaders. Actionable. https://conversations.actionable.co/thoughts/2017/08/ vertical-development-leaders

10. Fassinger, R. E., Shullman, S. L., & Stevenson, M. R. (2010). Toward an affirmative lesbian, gay, bisexual, and transgender leadership paradigm. *American Psychologist, 65*(3), 201–215.

11. Friend, R. (1991). Older lesbian and gay people. *Journal of Homosexuality, 20*(3–4), 99–118.

12. Sapolsky, R. (2004). *Why Zebras Don't Get Ulcers*. Henry Holt and Company.

13. NeuroLeadership Institute (2022, September 13). 5 ways to spark (or destroy) your employees' motivation. https://neuroleadership.com/ your-brain-at-work/scarf-model-motivate-your-employees

14. Sapolsky, R. (2004). *Why Zebras Don't Get Ulcers*. Henry Holt and Company.

15. Collinson, D. L. (2003). Identities and insecurities: Selves at work. *Organization, 10*(3), 527–547.

16. Kegan, R., & Laskow Lahey, L. (2009). *Immunity to Change: How to Overcome It and Unlock the Potential in Yourself and Your Organization*. Harvard Business Review Press.

Chapter 4

1. Meyer, I. H. (2003). Prejudice, social stress, and mental health in lesbian, gay, and bisexual populations: Conceptual issues and research evidence. *Psychological Bulletin, 129*(5), 674–697.

2. Shuster, S. M. (2021). *Trans Medicine* (p. 31). New York University Press.

3. Debruge, P. (2020, June 19). "Disclosure" on Netflix: Film review. *Variety*. https://variety.com/2020/film/reviews/disclosure-review-netflix-trans-lives-on-screen-1234642803

4. Gelwicks, A. (2020). *The Queer Advantage* (pp. 72–73). Hachette Book Group.

5. Gainsburg, J. (2020). *The Savvy Ally: A Guide for Becoming a Skilled* LGBTQ+ *Advocate* (p. 16). Rowman & Littlefield.

6. Collinson, D. (2003). Identities and insecurities: Selves at work. *Organization, 10*(3), 527–547.

7. Beeharilal, D. (2020, October 5). Code-switching and identity: Embracing

an intentional approach. Forbes. www.forbes.com/sites/forbescoachescoun cil/2020/10/05/code-switching-and-identity-embracing-an-intentional-ap proach/?sh=2ed0a9cb32ae

8. Longo, F. D. (2020). Companioning LGBTQ+ Clients on Their Developmental Journeys. 1. Unpublished.

9. Gelwicks, A. (2020). *The Queer Advantage* (p. x). Hachette Book Group.

10. Gainsburg, J. (2020). *The Savvy Ally: A Guide for Becoming a Skilled LGBTQ+ Advocate* (p. 19). Rowman & Littlefield.

11. Hendel-Giller, R. (2017, August). Vertical Development for Leaders. Actionable. https://conversations.actionable.co/thoughts/2017/08/ vertical-development-leaders

12. Longo, F. D. (2020). Companioning LGBTQ+ Clients on Their Developmental Journeys. 2. Unpublished.

13. Courage (2023). In Merriam-Webster.com. www.merriam-webster.com/ dictionary/courage

14. Pupius, D. (n.d.). Leadership Is Knowing When to Let Go. Range. www.range. co/blog/knowing-when-to-let-go

15. Collinson, D. (2003). Identities and insecurities: Selves at work. *Organization*, *10*(3), 527–547.

16. Martínez, S., Agoglia, J., & Levinger, M., (2013). Effective Leadership for a Complex World: A Developmental Approach. In *Changing Mindsets to Transform Security: Leader Development for an Unpredictable and Complex World* (L. Wells, T. C. Hailes, & M. C. Davies eds.) (pp. 53–80). National Defense University. https://ndupress.ndu.edu/Portals/68/Documents/ Books/CTBSP-Exports/Changing-Mindsets-to-Transform-Security. pdf?ver=2017-06-16-104715-250

17. Kegan, R. (1994). *In Over Our Heads: The Mental Demands of Modern Life* (p. 5). Harvard University Press.

18. Hendel-Giller, R. (2017, August). Vertical Development for Leaders. Actionable. https://conversations.actionable.co/thoughts/2017/08/ vertical-development-leaders

19. Yacovelli, S. (2019). *Pride Leadership: Strategies for the LGBTQ+ Leader to Be the King or Queen of Their Jungle* (p. 82). Publish Your Purpose.

20. Kegan, R. (1982). *The Evolving Self: Problem and Process in Human Development* (p. 261). Harvard University Press.

21. ibid. (18–19). Harvard University Press.

22. Kegan, R. (1994). *In Over Our Heads: The Mental Demands of Modern Life* (p. 5). Harvard University Press.

23. Rock, D. (2008). SCARF: A brain-based model for collaborating with and influencing others. *NeuroLeadership*. https://schoolguide.casel.org/uploads/ sites/2/2018/12/SCARF-NeuroleadershipArticle.pdf

24. Grant, A. (2021). *Think Again: The Power of Knowing What You Don't Know* (p. 4). Viking.

25. Conron, K. J., Goldberg, S. K., & O'Neill, K. (2020, October 1). *Religiosity among LGBT Adults in the US*. Williams Institute. https://williamsinstitute. law.ucla.edu/wp-content/uploads/LGBT-Religiosity-Oct-2020.pdf

26. Grant, A. (2021). *Think Again: The Power of Knowing What You Don't Know*. Viking.

27. ibid.

28. Gavatorta, S. (2017). *In Defense of Adversity: Turning Your Toughest Challenges into Your Greatest Success*. Richter Publishing LLC.

29. Isom, D., Daniels, C., & Savage, B. (2022, June 28). What everyone can learn from leaders of color. *Stanford Social Innovation Review*. https://ssir.org/ articles/entry/what_everyone_can_learn_from_leaders_of_color

Chapter 5

1. Garvey Berger, J., & Johnston, K. (2015). *Simple Habits for Complex Times: Powerful Practices for Leaders*. Stanford Business Books.

2. Helsing, D., & Lahey L. (2010). The Evolving Leader: When Development Yields Transformation. In Kram, K., Hall, T., & Bunker, K. (eds.), *The Missing Ingredient for Extraordinary Leadership: Filling the Gaps in Senior Executive Development*, pp. 69–94. Jossey-Bass.

3. Helsing, D., & Howell, A. (2014). Understanding leadership from the inside out: Assessing leadership potential using constructive-developmental theory. *Journal of Management Inquiry*, *23*(2), 186–204.

4. Bass, B. M. (1990). From transactional to transformational leadership: Learning to share the vision. *Organizational Dynamics*, *18*(3), 19–31.

5. ibid.

6. Edmonson, A. (2020, July 2). Psychological safety, emotional intelligence, and leadership in a time of flux. McKinsey & Company. www.mckinsey.com/ featured-insights/leadership/psychological-safety-emotional-intelligence-and-leadership-in-a-time-of-flux

7. Heifetz, R. A., & Linsky, M. (2002, June 1). A survival guide for leaders. *Harvard Business Review*, *80*, 65–74.

8. Finn, P., Mysore, M., & Usher, O. (2020, November 2). When nothing is normal: Managing in extreme uncertainty. McKinsey & Company. www.mckinsey.com/capabilities/risk-and-resilience/our-insights/ when-nothing-is-normal-managing-in-extreme-uncertainty

9. Blanchard (n.d.). SLII®. Powering Inspired Leaders™. www.kenblanchard. com/our-content/programs/slii

10. Schermerhorn, J. R. (1997). Situational leadership: Conversations with Paul Hersey. *Mid-American Journal of Business*, *12*(2), 5–6.
11. Gelwicks, A. (2020). *The Queer Advantage* (p. x). Hachette Book Group.
12. George, B., & George, W. W. (2003). *Authentic Leadership: Rediscovering the Secrets to Creating Lasting Value* (p. 11). Wiley.
13. ibid.
14. ibid.
15. Hess, E. (2018, January 16) An MBA student's toolkit for the smart machine age. *Financial Times*. www.ft.com/content/9d9f76c0-422e-11e7-82b6-896b95f30f58
16. Edmondson, A. C. (2018, November 14). How fearless organizations succeed. Strategy + Business. www.strategy-business.com/article/How-Fearless-Organizations-Succeed
17. Anderson, D., & Ackerman Anderson, L. (2013). Leadership Breakthrough: Meeting the Transformational Challenges of the 21st Century Security Environment. In Wells, L., Hailes, T. C., & Davies, M. C. (eds.) *Changing Mindsets to Transform Security: Leader Development for an Unpredictable and Complex World*, pp. 25–52 (p. 31). National Defense University. https://ndupress.ndu.edu/Portals/68/Documents/Books/CTBSP-Exports/Changing-Mindsets-to-Transform-Security.pdf?ver=2017-06-16-104715-250
18. Heifetz, R., & Laurie, D. L. (2001, December 1). The work of leadership. *Harvard Business Review*. https://hbr.org/2001/12/the-work-of-leadership

Chapter 6

1. Dromgoole, J. (2021). *Out to Lead: Shaping Queer Leadership* (p. 12). New Degree Press.
2. Fram, B. (2018, May 5). Commitment to serve—SSgt Sabrina Bruce. SPARTA. https://spartapride.org/warriors-of-sparta-ssgt-sabrina-bruce
3. Collinson, D. L. (2003). Identities and insecurities: Selves at work. *Organization*, *10*(3), 527–547.
4. Kegan, R., & Laskow Lahey, L. (2016). *An Everyone Culture: Becoming a Deliberately Developmental Organization* (p. 1). Harvard Business Review Press.
5. Fram, B. (2020, June 22). A command transition. Inkstick. https://inkstickmedia.com/a-command-transition
6. Kegan, R., Lahey, L., Miller, M., & Fleming, A. (2014, April 1). Making business personal. *Harvard Business Review*, *92*(4), 44.
7. Gelwicks, A. (2020). *The Queer Advantage* (p. 88). Hachette Book Group.

Chapter 7

1. Brown, R. T. (1989). Creativity: What Are We to Measure? In J. A. Glover, R. R. Ronning, & C. R. Reynolds (eds.), *Handbook of Creativity*, pp. 3–32. Plenum Press.
2. Gelwicks, A. (2020). *The Queer Advantage* (p. 6). Hachette Book Group.
3. Gelwicks, A. (2020). *The Queer Advantage* (p. 16). Hachette Book Group.
4. Defense Visual Information Distribution Service (2021, June 9). DoD LGBT Pride Ceremony 2021 [Video file]. www.dvidshub.net/video/800417/dod-lgbt-pride-ceremony-2021 (at time 36:45).
5. Heifetz, R. (1998). *Leadership without Easy Answers*. Harvard University Press.
6. Anderson, D., & Ackerman Anderson, L. (2013). Leadership Breakthrough: Meeting the Transformational Challenges of the 21st Century Security Environment. In Wells, L., Hailes, T. C., & Davies, M. C. (eds.) *Changing Mindsets to Transform Security: Leader Development for an Unpredictable and Complex World*, pp. 25–52 (p. 41). National Defense University. https://ndupress.ndu.edu/Portals/68/Documents/Books/CTBSP-Exports/Changing-Mindsets-to-Transform-Security.pdf?ver=2017-06-16-104715-250
7. ibid.

Chapter 8

1. Kegan, R. (1994). *In Over Our Heads: The Mental Demands of Modern Life*. Harvard University Press.
2. Dweck, C. (2006). *Mindset: The New Psychology of Success*. Random House.
3. Gelwicks, A. (2020). *The Queer Advantage* (pp. 73–74). Hachette Book Group.
4. American Psychological Association (2012, January 1). Building your resilience. www.apa.org/topics/resilience/building-your-resilience
5. Duckworth, A. L., Peterson, C., Matthews, M. D., & Kelly, D. R. (2007). Grit: Perseverance and passion for long-term goals. *Journal of Personality and Social Psychology*, 92(6), 1087–1101.
6. American Psychological Association (2012, January 1). Building your resilience. www.apa.org/topics/resilience/building-your-resilience

Chapter 9

1. IIC Partners (2014, February 5). Most desired trait by companies seeking senior executives is ability to motivate and lead others. https://iicpartners.com/media-center/most-desired-trait-by-companies-seeking-senior-exe
2. Joiner, B., & Josephs, S. (2007). *Leadership Agility: Five Levels of Mastery for Anticipating and Initiating Change*. John Wiley & Sons, Inc.

3. Cook, T. (2014, October 30). Tim Cook speaks up. Bloomberg. www.bloom berg.com/news/articles/2014-10-30/tim-cook-speaks-up#xj4y7vzkg

4. ibid.

Chapter 11

1. Phillips, K. W. (2014). How diversity works. *Scientific American, 311*(4), 42–47.

2. ibid.

3. Hart, B. H. L. (1991). *Strategy* (p. 354). Plume.

4. Miller, C. (2021). Inclusion: The power in diversity. *Journal of Character and Leadership Development, 8*(1). https://jcldusafa.org/index.php/jcld/article/view/52

5. Jones, J. (2022, January 10). Americans reading fewer books than in past. Gallup. https://news.gallup.com/poll/388541/americans-reading-fewer-books-past.aspx

6. Gainsburg, J. (2020). *The Savvy Ally: A Guide for Becoming a Skilled* LGBTQ+ *Advocate* (p. 2). Rowman & Littlefield.

7. Brown, J. (2022, August 4). Uncertain times call for a new type of leadership. Fast Company. www.fastcompany.com/90773295/uncertain-times-call-for-a-new-type-of-leadership

8. Gainsburg, J. (2020). *The Savvy Ally: A Guide for Becoming a Skilled* LGBTQ+ *Advocate* (p. 4). Rowman & Littlefield.

9. Sinek, S. [TEDxPugetSound]. How great leaders inspire action [Video file]. TED. www.ted.com/talks/simon_sinek_how_great_leaders_inspire_action/c

10. Badgett, M. V. L. (2020). *The Economic Case for* LGBT *Equality* (p. 130). Beacon Press.

11. Larson, E. (2017, September 21). *New Research: Diversity + Inclusion = Better Decision Making At Work.* Forbes. www.forbes.com/sites/eriklarson/2017/09/21/new-research-diversity-inclusion-better-decision-making-at-work/?sh=3f183714cbfa

12. Alexander, M. (2021, September 3). 5 ways diversity and inclusion help teams perform better. CIO. www.cio.com/article/189194/5-ways-diversity-and-inclusion-help-teams-perform-better.html

13. Miller, C., (2021). Inclusion: The power in diversity. *Journal of Character and Leadership Development, 8*(1). https://jcldusafa.org/index.php/jcld/article/view/52

14. https://pflag.org/about-us

Chapter 12

1. Rock, D., & Grant, H. (2016, November 4). Why diverse teams are smarter. *Harvard Business Review.* https://hbr.org/2016/11/why-diverse-teams-are-smarter
2. Schindler, J. (2019, April 17). Cognitive bias: Human brains are only human. Forbes. www.forbes.com/sites/forbescoachescouncil/2019/04/17/cognitive-bias-human-brains-are-only-human/?sh=7a8483c677be
3. Moskowitz, G. (2019, April 17). Are we all inherently biased? Lehigh University. www1.lehigh.edu/research/consequence/are-we-all-inherently-biased
4. Greenwald, A. G., & Calvin, K. L. (2020). Implicit social cognition. *Annual Review of Psychology, 71,* 419–445.
5. Baldock, K. (2014). *Walking the Bridgeless Canyon: Repairing the Breach between the Church and the* LGBT *Community* (p. 39). CanyonWalker Press.
6. Thoroughgood, N., Sawyer, K., & Webster, J. R. (2020, March 1). Creating a trans-inclusive workplace. *Harvard Business Review.* https://hbr.org/2020/03/creating-a-trans-inclusive-workplace
7. Gainsburg, J. (2020). *The Savvy Ally: A Guide for Becoming a Skilled* LGBTQ+ *Advocate* (p. 104). Rowman & Littlefield.

Chapter 13

1. Isom, D., Daniels, C., & Savage, B. (2022, June 28). What everyone can learn from leaders of color. *Stanford Social Innovation Review.* https://ssir.org/articles/entry/what_everyone_can_learn_from_leaders_of_color
2. Longo, F. D. (2020). Companioning LGBTQ+ Clients on Their Developmental Journeys. 1. Unpublished.
3. Gelwicks, A. (2020). *The Queer Advantage* (p. 146). Hachette Book Group.
4. Browne, J. (2014). *The Glass Closet: Why Coming Out Is Good Business* (p. 12). Harper Business.
5. Isom, D., Daniels, C., & Savage, B. (2022, June 28). What everyone can learn from leaders of color. *Stanford Social Innovation Review.* https://ssir.org/articles/entry/what_everyone_can_learn_from_leaders_of_color
6. Gavatorta, S. (2017). *In Defense of Adversity: Turning Your Toughest Challenges into Your Greatest Success* (p. 17). Richter Publishing LLC.
7. Iowa State University Center for Nondestructive Engineering (n.d.). *Glossary.* www.nde-ed.org/Glossary/letter/t.xhtml
8. It Gets Better Project (n.d.). Our Vision / Mission / People. https://itgetsbetter.org/blog/mission-vision-people
9. Dalio, R. (n.d.). Constantly Train, Test, Evaluate, and Sort People. Principles.com. www.principles.com/principles/faeb8045-7427-4b69-834c-9c3a8ca559c8

10. G. A. (2020, April 24). Magneto's entire backstory explained. Looper. www.looper.com/204425/magnetos-entire-backstory-explained

11. Allan, E. J., & Madden, M. (2008). *Hazing in View: College Students at Risk*. https://stophazing.org/wp-content/uploads/2014/06/hazing_in_view_web1.pdf

12. ibid.

13. Cohen, D., & Givnish, E. (2021, May 9). Grieving parents tell the stories of children lost to hazing. CBS News. www.cbsnews.com/news/grieving-parents-tell-the-stories-of-children-lost-to-hazing

14. Dromgoole, J. (2021). *Out to Lead: Shaping Queer Leadership* (p. 221). New Degree Press.

Chapter 14

1. Jacobs, D. L. (2016, September 23). Melissa Harris-Perry on expanding the definition of blackness. Plus. www.hivplusmag.com/activism/2016/9/23/melissa-harris-perry-expanding-definition-blackness

2. Dromgoole, J. (2021). *Out to Lead: Shaping Queer Leadership* (p. 201). New Degree Press.

3. OpenID (2023, March 29). *ChatGPT* (version 3.5) [Large language model]. https://chat.openai.com/auth/login

4. Yacovelli, S. (2019). *Pride Leadership: Strategies for the LGBTQ+ Leader to Be the King or Queen of Their Jungle* (p. 219). Publish Your Purpose.

5. Gainsburg, J. (2020). *The Savvy Ally: A Guide for Becoming a Skilled LGBTQ+ Advocate* (p. 2). Rowman & Littlefield.

6. Gainsburg, J. (2020). *The Savvy Ally: A Guide for Becoming a Skilled LGBTQ+ Advocate* (p. 4). Rowman & Littlefield.

7. Ingraham, C. (2015, September 22). The surprising geography of American left-handedness. *Washington Post*. www.washingtonpost.com/news/wonk/wp/2015/09/22/the-surprising-geography-of-american-left-handedness